Ernestine L. Rose

Ernestine L. Rose

To Change a Nation

Joyce B. Lazarus

HAMILTON BOOKS
AN IMPRINT OF
ROWMAN & LITTLEFIELD
Lanham • Boulder • New York • London

Published by Hamilton Books
An imprint of The Rowman & Littlefield Publishing Group, Inc.
4501 Forbes Boulevard, Suite 200, Lanham, Maryland 20706
www.rowman.com
86-90 Paul Street, London EC2A 4NE, United Kingdom

British Library Cataloguing in Publication Information Available

Library of Congress Cataloging-in-Publication Data

Names: Lazarus, Joyce Block, author.
Title: Ernestine L. Rose : to change a nation / Joyce B. Lazarus.
Description: Lanham : Hamilton Books, an imprint of Rowman & Littlefield, [2022]
| Includes bibliographical references and index. | Summary: "Ernestine L. Rose: To
Change a Nation relates the life of Ernestine L. Rose (1810–1892), a fearless human
rights activist who fought for racial equality, women's rights and religious freedom.
As America continues to struggle to live up to its democratic principles, Ernestine
Rose's words are more relevant than ever"— Provided by publisher.
Identifiers: LCCN 2022023637 (print) | LCCN 2022023638 (ebook) | ISBN
9780761873426 (paperback) | ISBN 9780761873433 (epub)
Subjects: LCSH: Rose, Ernestine L. (Ernestine Louise), 1810–1892. | Women social
reformers—United States—Biography. | Feminists—United States—Biography. |
Women's rights—United states—History—19th century. | CYAC: Jews—United
States—Biography.
Classification: LCC HQ1413.R6 L39 2022 (print) | LCC HQ1413.R6 (ebook) | DDC
303.48/4092 [B]—dc23/eng/20220629
LC record available at https://lccn.loc.gov/2022023637
LC ebook record available at https://lccn.loc.gov/2022023638

♾™ The paper used in this publication meets the minimum requirements of American
National Standard for Information Sciences—Permanence of Paper for Printed Library
Materials, ANSI/NISO Z39.48-1992.

Contents

List of Illustrations

1. Ernestine Rose (1810–1892), holding a book, taken in 1856. *Schlesinger Library, Radcliffe Institute, Harvard University.*
2. *Engraving of Ernestine Rose from a daguerreotype. Collection of the Massachusetts Historical Society, 81.565. Used with permission.*
3. Lithograph of Ernestine Rose by Leopold Grozelier, 1856. Rose is holding a scroll, perhaps representing a petition or law. *Library of Congress LC-USZ62–52045.*
4. Frederick Douglass (1818–1895), c. 1847–1852, by Samuel J. Miller. *Original image at the Art Institute of Chicago.*
5. Sojourner Truth (1799–1883), 1864. *Courtesy of the Library of Congress.* https://www.loc.gov/item/rbcmiller001306/.
6. "The Champions of Woman's Suffrage," *Harper's Bazar*, June 12, 1869, 38. *Division of Rare and Manuscript Collections, Cornell University Library.*
7. Elizabeth Cady Stanton (1815–1902) and Susan B. Anthony (1820–1906), c. 1870. *National Portrait Gallery, Smithsonian Institution, Washington, DC. S/NPG.77.48.*

Acknowledgments

My interest in Ernestine Rose began several years ago as I thought about the many crises facing our nation: our democracy has been under siege, we lived through a violent insurrection on January 6, 2021 to overturn a democratic election, we are reckoning with systemic racism, and we are in the midst of a global pandemic. These crises led me to me to study American history, to better understand how human rights activists from an earlier century fought against social inequities and racism during turbulent times.

My daughter and son-in-law, Suzanne and Marty Gold, suggested that I study the Civil War era, because of the role played by our ancestor during this period. My great-great-grandfather, Emil Bloch, born in Strasbourg, France, immigrated to the United States in 1850 at the age of 23. Like many other immigrants, including Ernestine Rose, he was undoubtedly drawn to America because of its promise of freedom and economic opportunity. He lived in New York City (like Rose) and supported himself as a storekeeper. I knew that he met and married my great-great grandmother, Florence, in New York and that they raised six children. When the Civil War broke out, Emil Bloch was drafted and he served his adopted nation. He was a sergeant in the 55th Regiment of the New York State Militia, fighting for the Union. He engaged in combat at the Battle of Antietam, in Maryland, considered to be one of the bloodiest battles in American history, with over 22,000 casualties. Fortunately, he survived this war, which was fought to save the Union, preserve our democracy, and end slavery..

How did America become so far removed from its original founding principles? As I began to read about abolitionists, I came across the name of Ernestine L. Rose and read Yuri Suhl's biography of her, which piqued my curiosity. I found Paula Doress-Worters' collection of Rose's speeches and letters very enlightening and soon I wanted to write an updated biography of Rose. I began my research and purchased a subscription to nineteenth-century American newspapers related to the antislavery cause, which gave me a first-hand account of this period.

As the Covid-19 global pandemic surged in 2020, my in-person visits to libraries came to a halt. I am very grateful to the "army" of librarians ready to assist me online, as I soon became isolated and remained in my "bunker" for the next year and a half, taking breaks for long walks.

I owe a debt of gratitude to the following cheerful and helpful librarians who assisted me online and answered my interlibrary loan requests: Emily Cramton and Aliza Spicehandler, at Klau Library, Hebrew Union College in Cincinnati, OH; Ellen Shea, at Schlesinger Library, Radcliffe Institute, Harvard University, Cambridge, MA; Danielle Marie Nista and Michael Koncewicz at Special Collections, New York University; Kate Long at Special Collections, Smith College Library; Chris Glass at Boston Public Library; the Reference Services Staff at the Center for Jewish History, New York, NY; Cathy Balshone and Jenna Weathers at Newton Free Library, Newton, Massachusetts.

Throughout this project, Brooke Bures, Associate Editor at Hamilton Books, has been extremely helpful. I very much appreciate her assistance, as well as that of Jessica McCleary, Production Editor at Hamilton Books, for helping to bring this project to fruition.

I am grateful to my late aunt Ruth Hagel for information about Emil Bloch, to Jacqui Horwitz for her help, and to Jane and David Salstein for their valuable comments on a first draft of the introductory chapter. Most of all, I am grateful to my children, Suzanne, Marty, Michael and Tania, to my grandchildren Nora and Ari, for their encouragement and love, and to my dear husband, Carl Lazarus, whose careful copyediting, continual support and love made this book possible.

Introduction

In August 1887, a seventy-seven-year-old widow named Ernestine Rose, her hair white and curly, wrote a letter to Reverend Edward F. Strickland, a progressive American clergyman who had been corresponding with her in Brighton, England.[1] He was putting together a collection on women's rights and requested her autograph and photo. "I am very glad that you and your dear wife take an interest in reform movements," she began. "For over fifty years I have endeavored to promote the rights of humanity without distinction of sex, sect, party, country or color." She enclosed a photograph of herself and added that she was sending him a copy of a lecture she had given thirty-six years ago in Boston on the rights of women. Rose continued, "[This lecture, along] with many others of mine, is not in the general reports of the woman's movement. I hope you will like it."[2]

Rose must have been pleased to receive a letter from Reverend Strickland, expressing his recognition of her work. At the same time, she was saddened that American reform movements had apparently forgotten her. As a human right's advocate who had spoken out forcefully for decades in the United States and in Europe for the abolition of slavery, for religious freedom, women's rights and international human rights, Rose was considered the foremost female lecturer in America during the mid-nineteenth century, the "Queen of the Platform."[3]

Most Americans today have never heard of her. During the last decades of her life, a younger generation of activists overlooked her accomplishments. Yet she had been a pioneer in many movements, articulating the notion that all Americans were endowed with natural rights guaranteed by the Declaration of Independence and by the Constitution. Her passion was to see everyone—both women and men, regardless of race, religion or ethnic origin—possessing the civil rights promised by American democracy. To achieve this goal, she believed that individuals needed to participate more fully in democracy, "not taking religion, politics or social ideas secondhand from their 'pastors and masters,' but [instead] choosing principles of belief, government, and conduct for themselves."[4] She was a fearless spokesperson for human rights who confronted slavery, racism, anti-Semitism, xenophobia, sexism and other social ills pervading American society. Rose was far ahead of her time, like other forward-thinking intellectuals such as Frederick Douglass and Susan B. Anthony.

How, then, do we explain the omission of Rose's name from many history books, given her important role as a social reformer?[5] This book will explore the enigma of Ernestine Rose, provide some plausible explanations for her absence from history books and attempt to offer a new understanding of her contributions.

As an immigrant from a place as far removed geographically and spiritually from New York City as any place that could be imagined—the Jewish ghetto in Piotrkow, Poland—Ernestine Rose arrived in America at a moment of great economic and social upheaval, to begin her career as a human rights activist. She was a twenty-six-year-old married woman still learning to master the English language. Unlike other female reformers in antebellum America such as Angelina and Sarah Grimké, Lucy Stone, Susan B. Anthony and Elizabeth Cady Stanton, Rose was the only non-Christian, foreign-born woman. For this reason, she did not entirely fit in with others and she felt tensions within the women's rights and abolitionist circles, as nativism and anti-Semitism worsened in the United States, beginning in the 1850's. Lucy Stone, among other reformers, said that she looked "too Jewish."[6]

Rose, who had rejected her Orthodox Jewish upbringing without ever converting to Christianity, was unique among reformers as a proud freethinker and spokesperson for religious freedom. This was an era of widespread prejudice against Jews and other "infidels," as they were called, and her outspoken opinions put her at odds with the religious zeal of the American public as well as that of many activists.

Drawn to the Enlightenment ideals that American democracy promised, she believed in the power of language to bring about social change. Emancipation would become Ernestine Rose's watchword:

I go for emancipation of all kinds—white and black, man and woman. Humanity's children are, in my estimation, all one and the same family, inheriting the same earth; therefore there should be no slaves of any kind among them.[7]

Rose had a rational, logical mind and felt compelled to use it, even though her speeches brought her into direct conflict with the social norms of nineteenth-century America. She was a formidable reformer, advocating for rights long before Lucy Stone and Susan B. Anthony, at a time when the appearance of a woman on the public platform was an astonishing sight. As one scholar noted, her European experience "helped make her mind more finely tuned to the issues facing the activists than were most other activists' minds. Her mind worked theoretically . . . as [she] talked a pragmatic reform strategy . . . She argued for what she saw as self-evident facts: that no one . . . in the species deserved special privileges at the expense of another . . . "[8] Rose's uncompromising stance on social reform issues, her anticlerical views as well as her foreign accent estranged her from some women's rights activists who were trying to gain acceptance in mainstream America.

Rose was not the first Polish-born immigrant to contribute to the cause of American democracy. Thaddeus Kosciuszko, a Polish general, had answered the call from the Continental Army to fight for American independence. He had fought in the American Revolutionary War and had become a close friend of Thomas Jefferson.[9] Rose and Kosciuszko were both drawn to America because of its promise of freedom and equal rights, and both of them fought battles, though their battles were of a different nature. Fighting against bigotry and narrow-mindedness could be as challenging as fighting on a battlefield when you were outnumbered by your enemy.

If one word could capture the spirit of mid-nineteenth-century America and Europe, it would be "emancipation." With an expansion of the press and growing international struggles for rights, the ideals of freedom, justice and equality dominated this era.[10] A wave of political revolutions swept through Europe, particularly in 1848, with the goal of toppling monarchies and creating independent nation-states. Many Americans saw these European revolutions as democratic uprisings. Karl Marx published his *Communist Manifesto* during this same year, calling for the working class—the proletariat—to unite in its struggle against exploitation and oppression in capitalist societies.

Emancipation in America meant liberty as well as citizenship and enfranchisement. It was an aspiration for all of humanity and a call for freedom and rights among specific groups—women, workers and most notably Blacks, of whom about four million in 1860 were slaves. The United States was an experiment in democracy that had introduced bold ideas about human freedom and had awakened a yearning for emancipation at home and internationally. This American experiment rested on three political ideas—"these truths"—as Thomas Jefferson called them: political equality, natural rights and the sovereignty of the people.[11] The Declaration of Independence proclaimed:

> We hold these truths to be self-evident, that all men are created equal, that they are endowed by their Creator with certain inalienable rights; that among these are life, liberty, and the pursuit of happiness.

Despite its lofty ideals, by the mid-nineteenth century America as a democratic republic was in grave danger, torn apart by slavery, as one political crisis after another foretold the coming Civil War. As the nation acquired new territory following the Mexican-American War in 1848, divisions and animosity in Congress grew over the question of whether new territory should be slaveholding or free. The Fugitive Slave Act (1850) and the Kansas-Nebraska Act (1854) stoked national tensions over slavery and drew Abraham Lincoln out of his law practice and back into politics.

America struggled, and would continue to struggle to live up to its principles and "to create a society governed by reason, truth and fairness rather than by violence, prejudice and deceit."[12] Lincoln spoke of the national crisis in 1854: "[The Kansas-Nebraska Act] forces so many really good men amongst ourselves into an open war with the very fundamental principles of civil liberty—criticizing the Declaration of Independence, and insisting that there is no right principle of action but *self-interest.*"[13] The republic's founding words were becoming less and less a reality and more a travesty. Lincoln privately wrote about his despair for the nation: "As a nation, we began by declaring that *'all men are created equal.'* [Soon] it will read, 'all men are created equal, except Negroes, and *foreigners, and Catholics.'* When it comes to this, I should prefer emigrating to some country where they make no pretense of loving liberty—to Russia, for instance . . . "[14]

Rose was overlooked by historians for over half a century following her death in 1892. A journalist, Henry Lewis, brought her name back into the limelight by publishing a full-page article about her, titled "Ernestine Rose— First Jewish Advocate of Women's Rights," in the Jewish socialist newspaper, the *Forward,* on June 19, 1927. The first book-length biography of Rose was Yuri Suhl's *Ernestine Rose and the Battle for Human Rights*, which appeared in 1959. Suhl, a writer on secular Jewish subjects, wrote a lively and captivating study of Rose's life but frequently omitted citations linking his facts to sources. Since the mid-twentieth century, three scholars have published biographies which have provided a fuller account of Rose's life and contributions, while providing important primary sources.[15]

There are still many intriguing topics to explore and gaps that we need to fill in our knowledge, in order to better understand Rose's life and work. The three most recent biographies, by Carol A. Kolmerten, Paula Doress-Worters and Bonnie S. Anderson, are thoroughly researched and compelling accounts of Rose's accomplishments. These books emphasize Ernestine Rose's important role in the American women's rights movement, while giving less attention to her internationalism, her abolitionist work and her advocacy of secularism.

Recent studies of Rose raise new questions that this book will attempt to answer. How did Rose bring a unique perspective to international human rights, abolitionism, freethought, religious freedom as well as to women's rights? What role did her Jewish upbringing play in her career? Finally, how did her work relate to that of some other contemporary reformers and writers,

European and American, both Black and white? This book takes a closer look at Rose's speeches and letters set in their historical context, in order to better understand her place in history.

Rose considered herself a citizen of the world. She spoke five languages fluently[16] and had a network of social reform friends in Europe with whom she maintained contact. A transnational approach to Rose can allow us to highlight cooperation between American and European reform movements and give us new insight into Rose as an important social reformer.

Researching and writing about Ernestine Rose have been challenging because she did not keep written documentation of her speeches nor did she write a memoir, diary or autobiography. She mentioned this subject in an 1877 letter to Susan B. Anthony:

> Believe me, it would give me great pleasure to tell you all about myself and my past labors . . . [but] I could not undertake the task, especially as I have nothing to refer to. I have never spoken from notes; and as I did not intend to publish anything about myself, for I had no other ambition except to work for the cause of humanity, irrespective of sex, sect, country or color, and as I did not expect that a Susan B. Anthony would wish to do it for me, I made no memorandum of places, dates, or names.[17]

When Rose and her husband left the United States in 1869 to move to England, they gave no motive for their departure. They may well have left some important papers behind; we have no way of knowing if they did. At the time of Rose's death, there were no known surviving family members who worked to preserve her legacy nor was there a repository for her collected papers.

Omissions made in the historical accounts of nineteenth-century women reformers have added another challenge for researchers. Susan B. Anthony, Elizabeth Cady Stanton and Mathilda Joslyn Age, authors of the first volume of *History of Woman Suffrage,* published in 1881, a definitive account of the women's rights movement, left out Ernestine Rose's name from the list of nineteen pioneers to whom the book was dedicated. This was surprising, since Rose was one of the most prominent pioneers, whom Anthony and Stanton admired.

With the digitization of nineteenth-century newspaper articles and of many other historic documents, scholars have rediscovered some of Rose's speeches as well as several letters and articles written about her that had previously been overlooked. We can now fill in gaps where there had been omissions, and in so doing, bring many of her forgotten words back to life.

This book will examine what emancipation meant to Ernestine Rose as she played a role in multiple reform movements during her lifetime. Chapter

1 focuses on her Polish-Jewish upbringing, her education and early travel experiences in Berlin, Paris and London. How did they affect the trajectory of her life and her dedication to social reform? Each successive chapter examines her contributions to different reform movements. Chapter 2 deals with her earliest efforts to bring about social change in America; Chapter 3 discusses her abolitionist work; Chapter 4 concerns her women's rights activism; Chapter 5 discusses her international human rights work; Chapter 6 deals with her contributions to freethought and religious freedom; Chapter 7 concerns her work in Europe and America during the 1870's; the Epilogue discusses her last years and her legacy.

As we explore this fascinating and elusive woman, Ernestine L. Rose, we will shed light on the ways that her unique background as a freethinking Jewish immigrant contributed to advancing social causes while hindering her full acceptance by society and her recognition by historians. We will ponder, finally, Ernestine L. Rose's true place in American history and her legacy.

NOTES

1. Regarding Ernestine L. Rose's appearance, the editor of the *National Reformer* wrote of her in 1871: " . . . the good old lady with her white curls, her erect, healthy-looking body, her clear, distinct voice. . . . ;" cited in Sara A. Underwood, "Ernestine L. Rose," *Heroines of Free Thought* (New York: C. P. Somerby, 1876), 276.

2. Ernestine L. Rose, Letter to Rev. Edward F. Strickland, August 30, 1887, American Jewish Archives, Klau Library, Cincinnati, Ohio.

3. *Hebrew Leader*, May 21, 1869,1.

4. George Jacob Holyoake, "Eulogy for Ernestine L. Rose," August 8, 1892, London, England, cited in Paula Doress-Worters, ed., *Mistress of Herself: Speeches and Letters of Ernestine L. Rose, Early Women's Rights Leader* (New York: The Feminist Press, 2008), 358.

5. Ernestine Rose's name was omitted from several recent books on nineteenth-century American history, including: James M. McPherson, *Battle Cry of Freedom: The Civil War Era* (New York: Oxford University Press, 1988); Jonathan D. Sarna, *American Judaism: A History* (New Haven: Yale University Press, 2005); and Jill Lepore, *These Truths: a History of the United States* (New York: W.W. Norton, 2018).

6. Lucy Stone, Letter to Susan B. Anthony, November 2, 1855, in *Stanton and Anthony Papers*, microfilm, reel 8, frames 298–309, cited in Bonnie S. Anderson, *The Rabbi's Atheist Daughter: Ernestine Rose, International Feminist Pioneer* (New York: Oxford University Press, 2017), 93–94.

7. Ernestine L. Rose, "Speech at the Anniversary of West Indian Emancipation," August 4, 1853, Flushing, N.Y., cited in Doress-Worters, 150.

8. Sherry Ceniza, *Walt Whitman and 19th Century Women Reformers* (Tuscaloosa: University of Alabama Press, 1998), 169–170.

9. Thaddeus Kosciuszko (1746–1817) was the first foreign officer to come to the aid of the American cause.

10. Among many international upheavals, there was the Greek uprising in the Ottoman Empire (1821–1832), ending in Greek independence, the Polish November Uprising in tsarist Russia (1830–1831), crushed by tsarist troops and the French July Revolution in (1830) and June rebellion (1832), which codified popular sovereignty in France. The Revolution of 1848 in France did not bring about a durable democracy. See Holly Case, *The Age of Questions* (Princeton: Princeton University Press, 2018), 80.

11. Lepore, xiv.

12. Lepore, xiv.

13. Abraham Lincoln, "Peoria Speech," October 16, 1854, in *The Collected Works of Abraham Lincoln,* 9 vols. (New Brunswick: Rutgers University Press, 1953), 2: 255.

14. Abraham Lincoln to Joshua Speed, August 24, 1855, in *Collected Works,* 2:323.

15. Biographies of Ernestine L.Rose include: Yuri Suhl, *Ernestine Rose and the Battle for Human Rights* (New York: Reynal, 1959); Carol A.Kolmerten, *The American Life of Ernestine L. Rose* (Syracuse: Syracuse University Press, 1999); Paula Doress-Worters, ed., *Mistress of Herself: Speeches and Letters of Ernestine L. Rose, Early Women's Rights Leader* (New York: The Feminist Press, 2008); and Bonnie S. Anderson, *The Rabbi's Atheist Daughter: Ernestine Rose, International Feminist Pioneer* (New York: Oxford University Press, 2017).

16. Rose spoke Yiddish, Polish, German, French and English.

17. Ernestine L. Rose, "Letter to Susan B. Anthony," January 9, 1877, in Susan B. Anthony, Elizabeth Cady Stanton and Matilda Joslyn Gage, eds., *History of Woman Suffrage,* 4 vols. (Rochester, NY: Charles Mann, 1887), 1: 98.

Chapter 1

A Polish-Jewish Upbringing

"I am . . . a daughter of poor, crushed Poland, and the down-trodden and persecuted people called the Jews, 'a child of Israel.'"[1] With these words, Ernestine Rose would introduce herself in 1852 at the Third National Woman's Rights Convention in Syracuse, New York. Her passion for social justice had its roots in a city as far removed from modernity as any place imaginable—Piotrków, Poland. Born Ernestine Louise Susmond Potowsky[2] on January 13, 1810, in this administrative capital in the province of Lodz, formally called Piotrków–Tribunalski,[3] she was the daughter of one of the principal rabbis, "respected for his science, his virtue and, to some degree for his wealth."[4]

The girl who would grow up to be a passionate human rights advocate was raised in an oppressive political environment and in the highly restrictive conditions of a Jewish ghetto. How would she find the strength to overcome so many obstacles to her independence and to her intellectual growth? How would her Jewish upbringing influence her choice of career? Ernestine Potowsky Rose was always reticent about her personal life and her past. Furthermore, she wrote no diary, memoir or autobiography. This has left historians with more questions than answers, particularly about her Jewish upbringing and identity.

By examining Rose's speeches, letters and references to her past, along with the writings of some contemporaries, we can better understand her complicated relationship with her Jewish upbringing. Ernestine Potowsky spent her earliest childhood years and much of her adolescence in Piotrków, Poland. Since the end of the eighteenth century, Poland had already ceased to exist as a country because it was partitioned among three occupying nations with absolute monarchies: Prussia under Frederick William III, Russia under Catherine the Great, and Austria under Empress Maria-Theresa.[5] War, oppression and anarchy had given Poland no respite for much of the eighteenth century. General Thaddeus Kosciuszko, who had fought with the American colonial forces to win independence from Britain, led a desperate insurrection for Polish freedom that would fail, ending with his imprisonment.[6]

Piotrków was under the control of Prussia since the partition of 1793. The Jews, numbering about 2,000 in 1810—almost one half of Piotrków's population—were confined to a ghetto and subjected to harsh discriminatory measures. They faced the ever-present threat of blood libels and anti-Semitic pogroms, carried out both by the local population and by invading forces. During one pogrom in 1740, a mob destroyed their synagogue, which they would rebuild at the turn of the nineteenth century. Jews paid higher taxes than non-Jewish residents and were forced to pay a tolerance tax, in the event they were found in a "forbidden" neighborhood; they paid a protectorate tax for the right to practice a vocation, a wedding tax, a tax levied on kosher animal slaughter and a military service tax, to avoid serving in the military. They were not permitted to work in many trades, could not purchase land, lend money on interest or rent an apartment from a non-Jew. Periodically, Prussian authorities issued decrees to expel Jews from Piotrków. A hateful painting depicting the alleged ritual murder of a Christian child by a Jewish mob led by a rabbi was prominently displayed on the wall of the Bernardin Church until 1825, when Jews succeeded in convincing authorities to transfer it to Warsaw.[7]

Living as an observant Jew with laws that regulated every aspect of her life—from the food she ate, the clothes she wore, her prayers and rituals—and growing up under the harsh conditions and hostile environment in Piotrków, Poland, Ernestine Potowsky was understandably drawn from a very early age to the dream of a freer society. She recalled the moment when she had begun to think about this:

> I remember I was but a little child, hardly able to understand the import of words, that I had already listened to them who pronounced it the 'Republic of the United States of America' and even then, though entirely unable to appreciate the import, the nobility of it, yet somehow or other it touched a vibrating chord in my heart, and I thought, if I live to grow up a woman, O how I should like to see a *Republic!*[8]

As a rabbi's daughter, she was accorded a much broader education than other girls of her generation would have known. Her closeness to her father gave her an opportunity to study Hebrew and the Bible in depth and to hone her skills in arguing and interpreting its moral and ethical concepts. Her contemporary biographers concur that she had deep affection for her father, while omitting details about her relationship with her mother. "As a child, she was of a reflective habit," wrote one journalist who had interviewed her, "and though very active and cheerful, she scarcely ever engaged with her young companions in their sports, but took great delight in the company of her father, for whom she entertained a remarkable affection."[9]

Ernestine Potowsky's parents would have sent her to a *heder*, a Jewish school where, in addition to studying Yiddish, Hebrew and the Torah (the first five books of the Hebrew Bible), she would have also studied German, under a decree from Prussian authorities.[10] The Prussian occupation may have also introduced some modern ideas and secular subjects such as mathematics. An important part of her upbringing and education would have been the Judaic ethic of repairing and healing the world, *tikkun olam*—the ideal of social justice which she would espouse throughout her life. The prophets—in particular Isaiah, Amos and Micah—who proclaimed the brotherhood of man, have been a fundamental part of Judaism for thousands of years. These biblical prophets were revolutionaries who called on mankind to change its course, to oppose idols and to respond to injustice.[11] She would have absorbed the biblical injunction in Deuteronomy 16:20: "Justice, justice shall thou pursue." In one of her addresses at a women's rights convention, years later, she would make a reference to this Jewish concept in a resolution she introduced: "That we ask not for our rights as a gift of charity, but as an act of justice."[12]

Ernestine Potowsky was inquisitive and precocious. With a rationalist frame of mind, she questioned everything that she was taught. She felt a need to investigate causes, to apply reason and to pursue justice. These qualities revealed themselves at age five when she became indignant in school over being punished for having done something which no one had told her was forbidden by the rules.[13] Her father then agreed to tutor her at home. As a rabbi, he would have taught her to value argument as a way to understand biblical and Talmudic texts more deeply. This was in fact the method applied for centuries by Orthodox students studying the Bible and Talmud. Ernestine would have honed her skills in logical reasoning during their discussions.

The Jewish community in Piotrków, overwhelmingly Orthodox and living a segregated lifestyle, may have had some exposure to the Jewish Enlightenment, the Haskalah, at the time of Ernestine Potowsky's childhood, since they were living under Prussian occupation. In addition, there may have been some French influence in the city since Emperor Napoleon Bonaparte had control over a large part of Poland until 1815.[14] The Haskalah brought modern, secular ideas to Judaism. For its followers, it was possible to be an observant Jew while fully embracing secular culture and reason. This philosophy had gained many followers in Western Europe by the turn of the nineteenth century. Piotrków would not fully adopt Enlightenment principles in its Jewish schools until the mid-nineteenth century. Still, it is possible that Ernestine Potowsky, who read much more than other girls of her generation, might have been influenced by modern ideas that had made their way in the 1820's into occupied Poland.[15]

Potowsky's logical mind and rebelliousness brought her into conflict with her father and with their Orthodox faith. Orthodox practices severely restricted the intellectual horizons of women and included the daily prayer thanking God " . . . who has made me according to Your will," the alternative to a man's prayer, thanking God " . . . who has not made me a woman."[16]

Her concern for her father made her question his religious practice when she saw that his fasting was damaging his health:

Why do you fast this way, Father?

Because God wants it.

Well, because God makes you harm yourself and then you afflict us all, he cannot be good and therefore I do not love him![17]

She read the Bible assiduously and her continual questions were creating escalating tensions with her father. Unable to hide her thoughts or to dissimulate, she would ask "why" after almost every verse, to which her father would reply:

It is necessary to believe because God has spoken.

But how do we know that it is God who has spoken?

Tradition proves it.

But Father, isn't it what you have heard from men that you call tradition? Is one obliged to believe what one has not seen nor heard, especially when one cannot understand it?

A young girl need not understand nor reason about her faith, but must believe and obey.[18]

Her father was becoming more and more alarmed at his rebellious daughter's constant questioning of sacred texts, and their conflict reached a breaking point during her puberty, when she gave up her religious practices completely because they were not consistent with reason. She would later tell an interviewer that "being constantly told that 'little girls must not ask questions,' made her at that early day an advocate of religious freedom and woman's rights; as she could not see, on the one hand, why subjects of vital interest should be held too sacred for investigation, nor, on the other, why a 'little girl' should not have the same right to ask questions as a little boy."[19]

By the age of fourteen, she renounced her belief in the Bible and in the religion of her father, which, according to a biographer, "brought down upon her great trouble and persecution alike from her own Jewish friends and from Christians."[20] Her father had apparently reached the limits of his religious tolerance and their break would become inevitable. Potowsky would later comment on this painful rupture with her Jewish faith and community:

> She [referring to herself] was the same as every other human being born into a sect. She had cut herself loose from it, and she knew what it cost her, and having bought that little freedom, for what was dearer to her than life itself, she prized it too highly to ever put herself in the same shackles again . . . The moment a man has an intellectual life enough to strike out [on] a new idea, he is branded as a heretic.[21]

In 1825, Ernestine Potowsky's mother passed away, leaving her a large inheritance.[22] Soon after this, her father, hoping to bring his daughter back to their Orthodox faith and to silence her doubts by marrying her off, betrothed her without her consent to someone he knew. It was the custom for parents to arrange their children's marriages and for girls in their community to get married at the age of sixteen. The engagement contract stated that all of her inheritance would be given to her future husband if she did not carry out the terms of the agreement.

In despair, Potowsky realized at the age of sixteen that "marriage without love was a terrible thing, and she became resolved that nothing should force her into this hateful contract."[23] She undoubtedly also knew that married women led a very restricted life in Piotrków, with little opportunity to expand their minds. With determination, she chose a bold plan of action.

The account of what happened next, as told by her French biographer, may stretch our credulity. After pleading in vain with her fiancé that she did not love him and could not marry him, she resolved to break the marriage contract. Her fiancé filed a lawsuit to gain possession of her wealth and the case was pending before the tribunal at Kalisz, over ninety miles away. In the dead of winter, the young woman found the courage to go alone by sleigh to the courthouse to plead the case herself. The sleigh broke down along the way. The driver urged her to wait until the next day to continue. The determined young girl refused, pleading with him to find someone to repair it. Potowsky waited alone through the snowy night, wrapped in furs, until four in the morning, when repairs were completed. They were then able to resume their trip to Kalisz. Although not yet seventeen, she managed to convince the judge that she should not have to pay with her property for an engagement entered into against her consent.[24] Strange as this narrative may seem, there is plausibility in the story, since historians have written about other Jews who successfully petitioned state officials and judges for equal treatment before the law.[25]

More than twenty-five years later, she would mention her experience before the judge in Kalisz, giving more credibility to her personal saga:

I have known a case in a foreign land under despotic rule, pleaded by a woman. This was the case of a girl hardly seventeen, who had to go to law to rescue her property staked on such a [marriage] contract, which she could not and would not fulfill; and against all the laws of the land, she gained that cause. How came she to get it? Because she pleaded it, and called down the Justice of Heaven against the laws.[26]

Her choice of the expression, "the Justice of Heaven" was a surprising one for someone who had rejected religion. She may have said it because it had been part of her vocabulary for so many years and because it was appropriate at this largely conservative women's rights convention. Potowsky's unusual education and her childhood years spent studying and arguing with her father about biblical texts had likely given her precocious skills and self-confidence to plead her own case at a trial. Her faith in justice and in the power of an individual to change unfair laws would stay with her for the rest of her life.

Potowsky's success in Kalisz may well have suggested to her that she could speak out in public about other unfair laws and social conditions, in order to bring about change. She understood from her Jewish upbringing and from her experience in Kalisz that laws were powerful and could remedy unjust social practices. "We have hardly an adequate idea how all-powerful law is in form-ing public opinion, in giving tone and character to the mass of society," she would assert in 1851. In her lecture, "A Defence of Atheism," she would later add: "If I have no faith in your religion, I have faith, unbounded, unshaken faith in the principles of right, of justice, and humanity."[27]

Upon returning home after her trial, Potowsky found her father newly mar-ried to a young woman of sixteen, whose character did not harmonize with her own. Not wanting to force her father to take sides in the conflicts she was anticipating, she made the decision to leave home. As one biographer put it, "She longed for a wider field of action. She had youth, good health, and [an] abundance of energetic daring. She was determined to seek her fortune in the great world."[28] As for the large inheritance she had acquired, she would explain her decision to give most of it to her father and keep a small portion for herself: "Let me only figure out how to earn my living honorably. That's all I need. Wealth would encumber me, would corrupt me, would render me useless. Thus, I will abandon it."[29] It may seem surprising that Potowsky chose not to take very much of her inheritance money with her so that she could live more comfortably as she traveled on her own. Even as an adoles-cent, her strong ethical principles convinced her that money could be a cor-rupting influence.

She left at age seventeen for Berlin, a cosmopolitan city with a thriv-ing Jewish community and modern Enlightenment ideas. It was a three-hundred-mile journey for her to make in a coach on unpaved, filthy, pothole-filled roads. A new obstacle presented itself immediately upon her arrival: Prussian laws prohibited Jews from staying more than three days in a city without posting monetary bonds from a Prussian citizen or obtaining permission from King Frederick William III.

Just as she had managed to plead her case in Kalisz, she again defended her case before a magistrate in Berlin: "I am or am not capable of doing evil. If I am, then the punishment must fall on my head and not anyone else's, and if I'm not, I have no need to post bonds." Legend has it that the magistrate sent her to a minister who, not being able to resolve the issue, conducted her to King Frederick William III. The king agreed with her that the law was absurd and offered to baptize her to solve the problem. To this, Potowsky replied: "I thank you, Your Majesty, but I have not abandoned the trunk in order to attach myself to the branches. If my reason prevents me from being Jewish, it cannot allow me to become Christian."[30]

As improbable as this story seems, it may well have taken place. Although she could have obtained the permit without too much trouble by applying for it, Potowsky had already demonstrated by her earlier actions in Kalisz that she was outspoken and persuasive. She preferred to defend her natural rights as a human being and to protest against an unjust law, as she would continue to do for the remainder of her life. She also chose to not convert out of Judaism. Her experience in Berlin reinforced her belief that freedom of expression and religious freedom were inalienable rights of every human being. She would consider herself a freethinker, which would place her in a painfully marginal position in society.[31]

Potowsky spent two years in Berlin, center of the Haskalah, where Jews, now citizens, were no longer confined to a ghetto but instead mingled freely with non-Jews and engaged in more lucrative professions such as commerce and finance. The young woman furthered her education through lending libraries and perhaps book groups or salons—almost the equivalent of a university education for her era. To support herself during her travels required her entrepreneurial skills and ingenuity. She paid for a modest rented room with the inheritance money she had brought along and with proceeds from the sale of her new invention—a perfumed paper that dispelled room odors.[32] By the end of her two-year stay she had become fluent in German.

In Berlin she studied, not the Bible, but books about current issues, as she became focused on questions about social practices. Potowsky concluded that crime and other social ills were largely caused by ignorance and inequalities, which could be reformed.[33] Her Jewish upbringing would have contributed to her belief that "every human being has a tendency to do good," rather than being tainted with original sin, as some branches of Christianity teach.[34]

After leaving Berlin, Potowsky visited Holland and then France, where in 1830 she witnessed the July Revolution that brought about the overthrow of King Charles X, an absolute monarch, and the ascension of the "Citizen King," Louis-Philippe. Years later, when she returned to Paris, she wrote about the excitement she had felt as a girl when "[she] saw General Lafayette present Louis-Philippe to the people" from the window of the Hôtel de Ville.[35] Looking back on the hopefulness of that popular uprising, she remarked sadly that "nations learn very slowly, and the French . . . paid dearly for allowing themselves to be deceived after 1830 by the recommendation of Lafayette."[36] Louis-Philippe would be forced to abdicate during the Revolution of 1848. Louis-Napoléon, elected to the presidency that year, would seize power in December 1851 and restore an absolute monarchy to France. Her eye-witness view of historic events in France and her travels through Europe would make her strongly favor a republican form of government.

During her stay in Paris, she observed the French character while admiring the artistic and cultural riches of the city. She would later write: " . . . Paris, beautiful as it is, [does] not so much interest me as the social, the moral, the progressive Paris [interests me] . . . To me it speaks the language of universal brotherhood; it seems the capital of the world, the representative of mankind."[37] She would add, "Paris is the seat of learning, the center of the arts, sciences and civilization."[38] Potowsky would become a lifelong Francophile. Her internationalist perspective, formed in part from her stay in Paris and Berlin, and from later European trips, would broaden her understanding of human rights issues.

During her 1830 stay in France, Ernestine Potowsky learned of a Polish uprising against tsarist Russia and she headed to Poland to participate in the insurrection. She was forced to turn back after traveling 250 miles east to the Prussian city of Koblenz, when authorities threatened to imprison her.[39]

She traveled next to London, the largest city in Europe. "We passed through a very fine part of the country . . . with verdure and flowers," she would later write, " . . . until we reached London, and then all was one dense mass of fog and smoke. London is so vast and immense that it takes a day to go anywhere or see anything . . . Sight-seeing is the hardest labor that can be performed."[40] Now twenty years old, she continued her study of "men and laws" in England. Although she knew no English when she arrived there, she showed remarkable entrepreneurial skills. With the help of an English dictionary, she was able to persuade a pharmacist to market her perfumed paper and she would earn additional income by giving Hebrew and German lessons to the daughters of a duke.[41] Her linguistic ability and determination helped her to learn English—her fifth language—within a few years.

Observing British society, Potowsky would later write about the inequalities she had seen in London. She showed a growing preoccupation with economic and social injustice:

What can I say . . . on a subject so vast [London] . . . so teeming with glory and degradation, splendor and wretchedness, the highest cultivation and refinement, and the almost barbarian ignorance and rudeness, the immense wealth with all its pride, and the lowest depth of poverty with all its abjectness, and of the tyranny, oppression, apathy, indifference, and subservience and submission which the terrible misrule of such extremes must naturally engender?[42]

In London, she met an important social reformer who shared her ideals—Robert Owen. Potowsky's encounter with Owen would change the entire course of her life. He was then a sixty-one-year-old industrialist who had become famous for his New Lanark Mills in Lanarkshire, Scotland—a model of good working and living conditions for its 2,000 inhabitants. Owen banned child labor for children under ten, improved sanitation, housing and the work environment. He devoted special attention to developing excellent schools for children of all ages, emphasizing character development and including innovative ideas such as dancing and music. Importantly, he prohibited corporal punishment. His New Lanark Mills were so successful that they became a place of pilgrimage for social reformers and statesmen. Owen would become a forerunner of utopian socialist communities in England and America and a father of British socialism.[43]

When Ernestine Potowsky began attending his weekly lectures, he had recently created an organization called "The Association of all Classes of all Nations," in which he introduced his reform ideas. He wanted to apply his innovative notions about education and work to society as a whole, in order to reduce poverty, inequality and social vices. Robert Owen described in a pamphlet, "The Social Bible: an Outline of the Rational System of Society," how to achieve this goal. He was convinced that established religions had done great harm by inculcating in society the principle of original sin—the notion that men and women were by nature evil and had to be forced to go against their natural inclination in everything. Owen believed that character was formed early in life mainly by external circumstances, by what social scientists would later call "nurture," and that this happened against a person's will. He described it this way: "The constitution of every infant, except in the case of organic disease, is capable of being formed or matured either into a *very inferior* or a *very superior* being, according to the qualities of the external circumstances allowed to influence that constitution from birth."[44]

According to Owen, in order to create a society of moral, productive and happy men and women, parents and educators must raise both boys and girls following certain principles, including the following: "the best education, from infancy to maturity of the physical, intellectual and moral power of all the population; the absence of superstition, supernatural fears and the fear of death; the full liberty of expressing thoughts upon all subjects . . . and laws and institutions all in unison with the laws of human nature."[45]

Owen's belief in complete equality for all, "without distinction of sect, party, sex, country or color" harmonized with Ernestine Potowsky's own ideas, and his rejection of religion created an important bond between them. He would become a mentor for her and a father figure during her formative years, whom she would address in letters as "my dear and respected Father."[46] In later years, she would describe his reform views this way:

> The old, erroneous idea of the depravity of human nature is daily giving way to philosophical inquiries into the nature of the causes and influences that produce depravity, vice and misery; and in just proportion as this truth is perceived and the corresponding remedies applied, so is moral reform successful.[47]

Potowsky began taking part in Owen's Sunday gatherings where, after dance and refreshments, she listened to speeches and before long began giving speeches herself on Owenite doctrines.[48] Her appearance was striking: "slender, petite . . . with a beautiful forehead, sparkling eyes, [and] even, white teeth." Her most outstanding feature was her voice. "[It was] a voice with a pure tone, gifted with a flexibility that provided nuance of expression to her thoughts with never a false note or shrillness that might offend a musical ear."[49] Another observer also spoke of her "rich, musical voice, with just enough foreign accent and idiom to add to the charm of her oratory. As a speaker, she was pointed, logical, and impassioned. She not only dealt in abstract principles clearly, but in their application touched the deepest emotions of the human soul."[50]

She clearly made a positive impression on her first audience, since an onlooker wrote: "[Despite the fact that] thousands had gathered there and notwithstanding her slight knowledge of the English language, the good looks and enthusiasm of the girl made a good impression on the audience. She was thenceforth encouraged to speak again and again."[51]

Owen's lectures and pamphlets gave the idealistic young Ernestine Potowsky not only a model for a new society but, in addition, a direction for her to follow with a concrete notion about how she might contribute to reforms. Owen had written in a pamphlet titled, "The Catechism of the New Moral World":

> How is this new public opinion to be formed?
>   By friends of truth, who have sufficient moral courage to contend against popular error and extensive prejudice, coming forward to support public meetings, public lectures, public discussions, and . . . publications advocating the cause of truth in opposition to error, and by becoming members of an Association now forming to extend truth unmixed with error over the whole world.[52]

She was strikingly beautiful, had boundless energy and the ability to command an audience. "I have never spoken from notes," she would later write. "I made no memorandum of places, dates or names."[53] How did she find the courage to speak spontaneously, even as she was still learning to master the English language? Perhaps her upbringing, as the only child of a rabbi who had showered her with attention and who had engaged with her in endless discussions, had played a part in this.

At one of Owen's gatherings she met William E. Rose, "an Englishman of broad, liberal views," who shared her enthusiasm for Robert Owen's social ideals. Very little is known about William Rose's background. Born in England in 1813, he was three years younger than Potowsky. Although raised in a Christian family, he became a freethinker and atheist, who earned his living as a silversmith and jeweler. They both enjoyed singing and dancing, and would frequently sing together at Owenite events. They were later married by a civil magistrate, since they both believed that marriage was a civil, not religious contract, based on mutual esteem and love.[54] William Rose became her devoted and beloved husband, who shared his wife's egalitarian ideals. Her past experience as a member of a persecuted minority in Poland convinced both of them to seek out a country—America—where in the early nineteenth century they saw the greatest hope for bringing about real societal change.

How, then, would Ernestine Rose's Polish-Jewish upbringing influence the trajectory of her life? It is clear that her rejection of all established religion was complete. She would feel so estranged from religion throughout her life that she would stipulate in her will that "her body not be taken into any Chapel or Church," and she would fear, late in life, that "religious persons might make her unsay the convictions of her whole life when her brain was weakened by illness . . ."[55]

Historians disagree about the influence of Rose's Jewish upbringing on her career. One scholar expressed skepticism about the objectivity of Rose's French biographer, Jenny P. d'Héricourt, saying that d'Héricourt "highlighted and perhaps exaggerated the early and categorical nature of Rose's adolescent disavowal of religion" since this disavowal of religion harmonized with her own strong anticlerical views and with that of the freethinker journal that published her biography.[56] Another scholar described the influence of Rose's Jewish upbringing this way: "For her, it was all or nothing. She went from being an observant Orthodox Jew to repudiating every precept she had been taught."[57]

While questions remain about Rose's self-identification as a Jew, her speeches and writings show the importance she attributed to her Jewish origins, as in her "child of Israel" remark quoted earlier. Growing up as a member of an oppressed Jewish minority in Poland and focusing at an early age on discussions of ethical principles contributed to her passion for social justice.

Her upbringing drove her commitment to progressive causes and informed her choice of career as a social reformer.

Despite her rupture with religion, Rose retained elements of Judaism—particularly its ethical precepts and emphasis on justice. Her choice of a career would paradoxically mirror her father's vocation. One of her father's principal responsibilities as a rabbi was to educate and advise others on moral issues and matters of law. For this he had refused to take a salary, saying that he "would not convert his duty into a means of gain."[58] Rose, like her father, would devote her time and energy to educating others on matters of ethics, justice and laws. She would never charge a fee for the lectures that she gave for over forty years, not wanting to profit personally from her speaking engagements. She exerted herself, not as a "means of gain" but for this reason that she gave: "[I have] served as a volunteer soldier in the cause of Truth."[59]

The Hebrew Leader, a German-English New York newspaper, described Ernestine Rose in 1869 as "an ardent adherent of moral Judaism" and considered her to be a deist. *Archives israélites*, a French weekly newspaper, would call her "a Jewish champion of feminine emancipation." It would describe Rose in these terms: "The originality of this woman deserves to be highlighted to show that all generous causes, even the riskiest, find in Israel [Jews] champions and apostles who are devoted and persevering."[60]

Despite her disavowal of religious faith, Rose would defend Judaism and Jews throughout her life.[61] By not converting, she refused to remove the "taint" of Jewishness that marginalized her in society. As historian Ellen Carol DuBois wrote, "Her Jewishness was thus not something from which, ultimately, she was willing to remove herself."[62] Rose may be seen as a forerunner of the mainly secular Ashkenazi Jewish immigrants at the turn of the twentieth century in America who joined labor and socialist movements to advocate for social reform.[63]

Ernestine and William Rose arrived in New York City on May 14, 1836 with high expectations and strong resolve. Their resolve would soon be tested by the challenges of a young American republic mired in crises and at war with its very founding principles.

NOTES

1. Ernestine L. Rose, "Speech at the Third National Woman's Rights Convention," September 8, 1852, in Paula Doress-Worters, ed., *Mistress of Herself: Speeches and Letters of Ernestine L. Rose, Early Women's Rights Leader* (New York: The Feminist Press, 2008), 121.

2. According to a biographer, "Ernestyna" is a Polish name and "Louise" "was a popular German name in this period, used to honor Queen Louise of Prussia." See

Bonnie S. Anderson, *The Rabbi's Atheist Daughter: Ernestine Rose, International Feminist Pioneer* (Oxford: Oxford University Press, 2017), 12.

3. Paula Doress-Worters, ed., "Madame Rose: A Life of Ernestine L. Rose as told to Jenny P. d'Héricourt," *Journal of Women's History* 15, no. 1 (Spring 2003):1–12, ProQuest.

4. Doress-Worters, ed., "Madame Rose," 5, 11. Ernestine Rose's mother provided a large dowry, equivalent to roughly $500,000 in U.S. dollars today.

5. Lucy S. Dawidowicz, *The Golden Tradition: Jewish Life and Thought in Eastern Europe* (Boston: Beacon Press, 1967), 13.

6. Dawidowicz, 13.

7. Ben Giladi, *A Tale of One City: Piotrykow-Trybunalski* (New York: Shengold, 1991), https://archive.org/details/nybc314221.

8. Ernestine L. Rose, "Speech at the 1855 New England Anti-Slavery Convention," in Doress-Worters, ed., *Mistress of Herself,* 188.

9. L.E. Barnard, "Ernestine L. Rose," in Elizabeth Cady Stanton, Susan B. Anthony, Matilda Joslyn Gage, eds., *History of Woman Suffrage*, vol.1: 95, Gutenberg E-book.

10. Giladi, https://archive.org/details/nybc314221.

11. Mordecai M. Kaplan, *Judaism as a Civilization: Toward a Reconstruction of American Jewish Life* (Philadelphia: Jewish Publication Society, 1981), 462.

12. Ernestine L. Rose, "Debate at the Third National Woman's Rights Convention, September 9, 1852," in Doress-Worters, ed., *Mistress of Herself,* 126. I am indebted for this observation to Suzanne Griffel, in her unpublished paper, "Ernestine L. Rose, as Jew and Social Activist," May 30, 1986, American Jewish Archives, Hebrew Union College, Cincinnati, Ohio.

13. Doress-Workers, ed.,"Madame Rose," 5.

14. Prussia ceded a part of Poland to Napoleon Bonaparte in 1807 under the terms of the Treaties of Tilsit. See Giladi, *A Tale of One City*. France was the first European nation to emancipate the Jews and to give them full rights as citizens.

15. Iris Parush and Ann Brener, "Readers in Cameo: Women Readers in Jewish Society of Nineteenth Century Eastern Europe," *Prooftexts* 14, no. 1 (January 1994):1–23.

16. Yuri Suhl, *Ernestine Rose and the Battle for Human Rights* (New York: Reynal, 1959), 10.

17. "Madame Rose," 5.

18. "Madame Rose," 5.

19. Barnard, 95.

20. Barnard, 95–96.

21. *Proceedings of the Woman's Rights Convention held in Syracuse*, September 8, 9, and 10, 1852 (Syracuse, NY: J.E. Masters, 1852), 85–86.

22. "Madame Rose," 11.

23. Sara A. Underwood, "Ernestine L. Rose," *Heroines of Free Thought* (New York: C. P. Somerby, 1876), 262.

24. "Madame Rose," 5.

25. Giladi, https://archive.org/details/nybc314221.

26. Ernestine L. Rose, cited in *Proceedings of the National Woman's Rights Convention,* Cleveland, Ohio, October 5–7, 1853 (Cleveland: Grey, Beardsley, Spear, 1854), 104.

27. Ernestine L. Rose, "Speeches at the Second National Woman's Rights Convention," October 15 and 16, 1851, in Doress-Worters, ed., *Mistress of Herself,* 95; Ernestine L. Rose, *A Defence of Atheism: a Lecture Delivered in Mercantile Hall, Boston,* April 10, 1861 (Boston: J. P. Mendum, 1881), 21; See also Ellen Carol DuBois, "Ernestine Rose's Jewish Origins and the Varieties of Euro-American Emancipation in 1848," in Kathryn Kish Sklar and James Brewer Stewart, eds., *Women's Rights and Transatlantic Antislavery in the Era of Emancipation* (New Haven: Yale University Press, 2007), 279–296.

28. Underwood, 264.

29. "Madame Rose," 6.

30. "Madame Rose," 6.

31. "Freethought" is a viewpoint which holds that one's beliefs should be based not on authority, religion or tradition, but instead on one's own reason, logic and observation.

32. "Madame Rose," 6.

33. "Madame Rose," 6.

34. Ernestine L. Rose, "Speech at the Infidel Convention," May 4, 1845, in Doress-Worters, *Mistress of Herself,* 69.

35. Ernestine L. Rose, Letters, *Boston Investigator,* October 15, 1856, 1.

36. Letters, *Boston Investigator,* November 26, 1856, 1.

37. Letters, *Boston Investigator,* October 8, 1856, 1.

38. Letters, *Boston Investigator,* November 26, 1856, 1.

39. "Madame Rose," 6.

40. Letters, *Boston Investigator,* July 30, 1856, 1.

41. "Madame Rose," 6.

42. Ernestine L. Rose, "Travel Letter no. 2: Visiting Robert Owen," July 6, 1856, in Doress-Worters, ed., *Mistress of Herself,* 211.

43. Although Owen's experimental socialist communities were not very successful, he was credited with inspiring the development of trade unions and workers' cooperative societies.

44. Robert Owen, *The Social Bible: an Outline of the Rational System of Society* (London, H. Hetherington, 1840), 2.

45. Owen, 6.

46. Ernestine L. Rose, "Letter to Robert Owen, April 14, 1845," in Doress-Workers, ed. *Mistress of Herself,* 68.

47. *Mistress of Herself,* 133.

48. "Madame Rose," 7.

49. "Madame Rose," 4–5.

50. Barnard,100.

51. Moncure D. Conway, an American Unitarian minister and friend of Ernestine Rose, was quoted in Underwood, 265.

52. Robert Owen, *The Catechism of the New Moral World* (London: H. Hetherington, 1830), 12.

53. Ernestine L. Rose, Letter to Susan B. Anthony, January 9, 1877, in Stanton, Anthony, and Gage, eds., *History of Woman Suffrage*, vol. 1: 99, Gutenberg E-book.

54. Underwood, 266.

55. "Last Will and Testament of Ernestine Louise Rose," reproduced in Suhl, 289; Hypatia Bradlaugh Bonner, quoted in Suhl, 273.

56. "Madame Rose," 2–3. The French freethinker journal that originally published this biography was *Revue Philosophique et Religieuse* 5 (Paris: Bureaux de la Revue, 1856): 129–139.

57. Anderson, 14.

58. Barnard, 95.

59. Ernestine L. Rose, "Letter to the Editor," *Boston Investigator*, April 30, 1856, in Doress-Worters, ed., *Mistress of Herself,* 208.

60. *The Hebrew Leader* XIV, no. 6 (May 21, 1869): 1; "Un Champion israélite de l'Émancipation féminine," *Archives israélites*, 53 (1892): 317–318. The translation is my own.

61. See Chapters 5 and 6 of this book for examples of Rose's defense of Judaism.

62. Ellen Carol DuBois, "Foreword," in Doress-Worters, ed., *Mistress of Herself,* xix.

63. American Jewish Socialism arose, beginning in the 1880's, with the mass immigration of Jews from Russia and Eastern Europe. It was a response to persecution in Europe and to economic hardship on both sides of the Atlantic. See Lori D. Ginzberg, "The Heathen Wing: Reflections on Secular Jewish Traditions," *Bridges* (Summer 1998): 7–14.

Chapter 2

Breaking up the
Time-Hardened Soil

Ernestine and William Rose arrived in New York City in 1836, drawn like countless other immigrants to America as an experiment in democracy that held great promise. Just one year earlier a young French aristocrat, Alexis de Tocqueville, had published the first volume of his work, *Democracy in America*, after traveling for nine months in the United States. He noted both the hopefulness of American democracy and the greatest threats to its existence:

> Among the new things that attracted my attention during my stay in the United States, none struck me more forcefully than the equality of conditions. It imparts a certain direction to the public spirit and a certain shape to laws . . .
>
> The prejudice against Negroes seems to increase in proportion to their emancipation, and inequality is enshrined in mores as it disappears from laws. The influence of slavery . . . penetrates the master's very soul.[1]

De Tocqueville's observations captured the deep contradictions engrained in America: its promise of freedom and equality and the inhumanity of slavery and racial prejudice.

The Roses settled in the Lower East Side of Manhattan, a diverse immigrant neighborhood where William Rose opened a silversmith and jewelry shop, and sold cologne paper designed by his wife. They moved into an apartment above the shop, at 484 Grand Street, a few blocks from the East River. William Rose would provide both financial and emotional support for his wife throughout their life together as they became immersed in social reform.

The Lower East Side was not yet the teeming neighborhood of tenement buildings it would later become. New York City immigrants in the first half of the nineteenth century were largely from Great Britain and Germany. The Jewish population numbered only about 4,000, less than 2% of the whole. By the late nineteenth century, the Lower East Side would become a refuge for tens of thousands of immigrants from Eastern Europe, including a "Great Wave" of Jewish migrants fleeing the Russian Empire.[2]

City life in the 1830's was still primitive and the Roses' apartment would likely have been without indoor plumbing.[3] An engraving titled, "Broadway and Grand Street in 1830," shows two and three-story buildings along wide, nearly empty streets lined with graceful poplar trees. A later print, "Broadway between Howard and Grand Streets, 1840," shows two, three, and four-story buildings along Broadway, now teeming with pedestrians and horse-drawn coaches, reflecting an increased influx of immigrants and economic growth.[4]

New York had become by this time the largest city in the country. Life in Manhattan was hazardous and fraught with danger, with its residents regularly tossing their trash out on streets and with clean water only available from street pumps.[5] It was a city of stark contrasts: economic opportunity and abject poverty; a fertile ground for reformers yet mired in crises.

The Roses would have felt at home in the city's immigrant community and in the progressive atmosphere of New York, with its many reform movements—workers' rights, moral reform, temperance movements, freethought, women's rights and abolitionism. Workers' dissatisfaction with wages and working conditions led to numerous strikes—ten during the year of the Roses' arrival—and to riots. This unrest was a precursor to a financial collapse, the Panic of 1837, the worst American economic crisis before the Civil War.[6] The antislavery movement was beginning to accelerate during this same period, thanks in part to William Lloyd Garrison's widely read newspaper, *The Liberator.*

The time was ripe for change in America. This long-awaited change would begin with immigrants and Blacks, who were the first to challenge America's claims to democracy. They focused on slavery, racism and women's rights. In Boston, a Black abolitionist and women's rights advocate, Maria Stewart, was one of the first women to speak in public before a mixed-race and mixed-gender audience in 1832. She called for women's rights and for an end to slavery and oppression. "How long shall the fair daughters of Africa be compelled to bury their minds and talents beneath a load of iron pots and kettles?" she asked.[7] Frances Wright, an Owenite reformer and freethinker from Scotland, also gave speeches on women's rights and abolitionism, paving the way for Rose.[8] Ernestine Rose would later pay tribute to Wright's influence:

Frances Wright was the first woman in this country who spoke on the equality of the sexes. She had indeed a hard task before her. The elements were entirely unprepared. She had to break up the time-hardened soil of conservatism, and her reward was sure—the same reward that is always bestowed upon those who are in the vanguard of any great movement. She was subjected to public odium, slander and persecution. But . . . she had her reward—the reward springing from the consciousness of right, of endeavoring to benefit unborn generations.[9]

Rose might just as well have been speaking about herself, for she too would face hostility and hardened conservatism during the next thirty-three years, as she dedicated herself to the daunting task of trying to bring America closer in line with its principles. She was a young woman of twenty-six, still mastering the English language, who would address large audiences at a time when women rarely spoke in public.

Rose recalled decades later her first impressions of America:

> I doubt whether I should ever forget the sensations and emotions I experienced when I first placed my foot on the soil of a Republic; nay, more, the first Fourth of July that I spent here. Why, everything in nature appeared to change and become superior. The sun shone brighter; the trees looked more beautiful; the grass looked greener; the birds sang sweeter; all the beauties of nature became enhanced in my estimation, for I viewed them all through the beautiful rainbow colors of human freedom.

Rose, continuing her address, contrasted her first, glowing vision of America with the grim reality she soon encountered:

> Alas! I little knew then what I should experience if I remained longer . . . This country has sent forth to the world a great and glorious truth—that eternal truth of the equality of men . . . And yet, while that declaration is thus wafted . . . all over the earth, here, under its shadow, the children that had been born and brought up here are subjected to dark and bitter bondage. This country therefore stands before the moral consistency of the world, to be judged thereby.[10]

Unlike many social reformers inspired by their religious faith, Ernestine and William Rose found their inspiration for broad-based reform in the "self-evident" secular truths of the Declaration of Independence. Rose would express it this way:

> By human rights we mean natural rights, and upon that ground we claim our rights, and upon that ground they have already been conceded by the Declaration of Independence, in that first great and immutable truth which is proclaimed . . . 'that all men are created equal, and that therefore all are entitled to certain inalienable rights, among which are life, liberty, and the pursuit of happiness.'[11]

Rose understood the phrase, "all men are created equal" to refer to "all human beings." While these truths might seem "self-evident," they have long been a source of controversy, and societal change has always been

extraordinarily slow and difficult to achieve. The hurdles she needed to overcome in order to change entrenched attitudes and to reform laws were formidable. How did she intend to accomplish this? She would give this response:

> The answer is, by agitation—conventions and public lectures . . . Legislative
> bodies are not apt to do justice to any party . . . without the force of public
> opinion. Agitation to enlighten and form that opinion is the only means to obtain
> the desired end . . . 'Agitate! Agitate!' ought to be the motto of every reformer.
> Agitation is the opposite of stagnation–the one is life, the other death.[12]

As an orator, Ernestine Rose's method involved stirring up debate and
influencing public opinion through the power of logical reasoning and
eloquence. If her words provoked a strong emotional response—protests
and controversy—this was a positive sign, she felt, because it meant that
her speeches were effective and were hitting home.[13] Rose faced additional
obstacles as a freethinker, an immigrant and a woman. Anti-immigrant sentiment would grow in the decades following her arrival. Philip Hone, a wealthy
merchant and former mayor of New York City, in a diary entry written in June
1836, revealed his feelings towards immigrants:

> June 2. There arrived at this port, during the month of May, 15,825 passengers.
> All Europe is coming across the ocean; all that part at least who cannot make a
> living at home; and what shall we do with them? They increase our taxes, eat
> our bread, and encumber our streets, and not one in twenty is competent to keep
> himself.[14]

During the Roses' first year in America, a state legislator, Thomas Herttell,
introduced a married women's property bill into the New York Legislature.
Herttell was a freethinker who spent his career arguing for rights, including
religious freedom, women's property rights and universal suffrage.[15] This
gave Ernestine Rose her first opportunity to work for change. In New York, as
in most American states, when a woman married she lost all right to her property, as well as to her wages, inheritance and custody of her children. Within
a few months of her arrival in the United States, Rose began going door to
door, collecting names for a petition that urged passage of Thomas Herttell's
proposed property bill.[16] She later wrote about this experience:

> I sent the first petition to the New York Legislature to give a married woman
> the right to hold real estate in her own name, in the winter of 1836–37, to which
> after a good deal of trouble I obtained five signatures. Some of the ladies said
> the gentlemen would laugh at them; others, that they had rights enough; and
> the men said the women had too many rights already. . . . But no sooner did it

become legal than all the women said, "Oh! That is right! We ought always to have had that."[17]

It was arduous work to obtain the passage of a new law. By sending petitions to the legislature year after year, Rose and other activists would finally succeed, twelve years later, in having a law passed that gave a married woman the right to hold real estate in her own name. Ernestine Rose is credited with being the first woman in the United States to petition a state legislature for women's rights—a remarkable feat, given that she was a newly arrived immigrant.[18] "This was not much, to be sure," she later wrote, "for at best it was only for the favored few, and not for the suffering many. But it was a beginning, and an important step, for it proved that a law had to be altered, and some others might need it just as much."

Her achievement involved changing the mindset of a large number of men and women. She compared this undertaking to that of a physician treating a patient:

> It was indeed discouraging, for the most hopeless condition is that when a patient loses all sensation of pain and suffering. But by depicting their condition to themselves, by holding before them the mirror of facts, it had the wholesome effect of an irritant, and roused to some extent at least their dormant energies.[19]

Rose began to speak in public outside the freethought community one year after her arrival in America. At a large public meeting held to discuss improving public education, Reverend Robert Breckenridge digressed from the subject to harangue those he stigmatized as "infidels." A New York newspaper, the *Beacon,* reported what occurred next:

> A young, beautiful and interesting Lady with uncovered head and fine flowing locks arose in the gallery opposite the speaker, saying that it [was] very painful for her, being a woman and foreigner, to intrude upon the audience, and nothing but a sense of duty and regard for truth induced her to rise. . . . she humbly begged permission of the Chairman to ask the gentleman (Breckenridge) . . . a question.[20]

Rose then took the occasion to call the pastor to order for overlooking the important subject of the meeting—public education. "This bold innovation upon the hitherto unquestioned prerogatives of the clergy at once caused a tremendous excitement," reported the journalist. "Loud cries—'Throw her down!' 'Drag her out!' 'She's an Infidel!'—resounded in all parts of the building. She, however, remained calm and composed while the tumult lasted, and after quiet was restored, continued her remarks, which made a deep impression upon those present."[21]

Within a few years, the Roses joined the freethought community in commemorating Thomas Paine's birthday, an annual January 29th event that had
begun in 1827. Freethinkers believed that Paine, a Founding Father whose
ideas had greatly contributed to the Declaration of Independence and the
American Constitution, had been denied his place in history because of
his rejection of established religion.[22] Paine's pamphlet, "Common Sense,"
which had advocated that American colonists fight for an independent, egalitarian government, was a powerfully persuasive document that had made the
American Revolution inevitable. When someone told Ernestine and William
Rose that "ladies were not admitted to the [Paine] dinner," the Roses organized an alternate Paine celebration in 1840, a tradition that would continue
for the next twenty-one years until it ended with the Civil War. Ernestine
Rose would become president of the Paine Society and would give lectures
at annual celebrations.[23]

William Rose gave two toasts at the 1840 Paine dinner: "Our Country—
While we give it our patriotic support, let it not be at the sacrifice of that
philanthropy and justice due to all mankind as brethren," and "Health to the
sick, honor to the brave, success to the lover and freedom to the slave." The
Boston Investigator refers to a speech made by Ernestine Rose that evening
that was unfortunately not recorded. [24]

Rose took a break from other public speaking engagements from 1839 to
1843, most likely because of childbirth. Her French biographer noted that
"she had two children that she cherished, nurtured with her milk, and whom
she tragically lost at a very early age."[25] She confided these details to her
biographer but never made a reference to this personal loss in any of her public addresses. In a letter she wrote one year later to Robert Owen, she shared
her private feelings with him: "My health since you left us has not been good.
I had several quite severe attacks of depression of mind. Mr. Rose wishes me
to go to Washington. He and our friends think that the change of climate and
scenery and society will be beneficial to me . . . "[26]

In the spring of 1844, Ernestine Rose, thirty-four years old, joined Ralph
Waldo Emerson, Henry David Thoreau and other reformers as participants in
a Sunday lecture series held at Amory Hall in Boston. Rose stood out from
all other speakers as the only woman, foreigner and non-Protestant. To her
audience, she was "exotic" with her Polish accent and dark, curly hair. A journalist later wrote of her: "Mrs. Rose was in her prime—an excellent lecturer,
liberal, eloquent, witty, and we must add, decidedly handsome . . . Her . . .
intelligent-looking and expressive countenance and black glossy curls denote
intellect and beauty."[27]

Boston in the 1840's was a center of social, political and religious ferment
that would stir the entire nation. Writers, philosophers and social reformers
were responding to crises created by the industrial revolution—to child labor,

unsanitary conditions in factories, long hours and low wages for workers. Some were advocating a retreat from cities to utopian communities where shared manual labor and vegetarianism replaced the practice of harnessing animals for farm work. Ralph Waldo Emerson railed against the "hypocrisy, imperfection, ignorance, oppression and immorality of society." He championed women's suffrage and spoke passionately against slavery.[28] Henry David Thoreau was skeptical of traditional religion and sought a new relation to the world in solitude, amidst nature, turning to "the resources of the self, the only realm where true liberation might be gained."[29]

The topics of the Amory Hall lectures in 1844 were very varied. William Lloyd Garrison, though a well-known abolitionist, spoke during his lecture about reforming the Protestant Church. Charles Lane and Charles Dana spoke about Fruitlands and Brook Farm, two utopian communal experiments in Massachusetts, while Wendell Phillips spoke about the immorality of slavery and the urgent need to end this institution. Both Emerson and Thoreau gave lectures on their individualistic philosophy, Transcendentalism, which opposed experiments in communal living in favor of a more solitary life. True reform, Emerson wrote in his 1841 essay, "Self-Reliance," began with individual moral behavior, with pursuing one's own thoughts rather than adhering to public norms.[30]

Ernestine Rose's Amory Hall lecture on March 24, 1844 was titled, "Social Reform."[31] Although there is no record of her speech, there are excerpts from one she gave a few months later on this same subject, in which she criticized the adverse effects of capitalism:

> The great falsehood at the foundation of society is that man is an individual—that his rights, interests, and immunities are separate from the rights, interests and immunities of others . . . From this great error of man's individuality the earth has been cut up. Separate possessions and hostile interests have been produced. The cunning have got the earth and the powerful live upon the produce of the poor man.[32]

As an Owenite, Rose argued that capitalism and private property led to stark inequalities in society, which socialism could remedy. While the Roses donated a portion of their income to the Owenite community of Skaneateles in New York, they chose nevertheless to earn their living from private enterprise and to not move out of New York City. Their decision to remain in New York suggests that Ernestine and William Rose felt that the United States was not yet ready in the 1840's to carry out the utopian socialist ideals professed by Robert Owen.

Rose elaborated on her social reform views in a speech she gave in 1845. She spoke at a freethought convention which she had renamed the "Infidel" Convention, to proudly affirm a term that others had used as an insult:

> Tell me, my friends, will the preaching, 'thou shalt love thy neighbor as thyself,' as long as isolated interests exist, avail us anything? So long as the precept exists—'everyone for himself, and some supernatural power for us all'—how much can you love your neighbor? There is a great deal of poverty in the world; but is there any necessity for poverty? . . . There is ten times more in the world than would maintain all in yet unknown luxury. Yet how much misery there is in our midst; not because there is not enough, but owing to the misdirection of it. Those who create the most get the least; those who build the largest castles, often have not where to lay their heads; and then we say that man is bad by nature, because if he has not a crumb to eat, he will take some from his neighbor.[33]

Rose's speech anticipated the growth of labor unions and of workers' demands for a fair, livable wage—an issue relevant to both capitalist and socialist societies. Later in the nineteenth century, workers would organize labor unions that supported collective bargaining, including the National Labor Union (1866), the first national American labor federation, which pressed for labor reforms and an eight-hour working day.

Rose delivered her address on workers' rights three years before Karl Marx published his *Communist Manifesto* (1848), which blamed capitalism for favoring the interests of a small, wealthy minority at the expense of the majority of laborers, members of an impoverished working class. Her reform ideas, outside of mainstream American thinking during much of her lifetime, have become increasingly relevant since the twentieth century, in debates over raising the minimum wage and having a guaranteed wage plan.

While Rose was speaking about workers' rights, Protestant churches, particularly evangelical ones, often had a very different message. Congregants heard some pastors say that the Panic of 1837 had been God's judgment on them and that membership in unions should be avoided.[34] Rose, in contrast, felt that poor, unsanitary working conditions and unfair, degrading treatment of workers by their employers were the true causes of poverty and crime. She rejected the notion that human nature was intrinsically bad. While speakers at the Amory Hall lectures disagreed on many issues, they all agreed that reason and private conscience, rather than the dictates of the church or public opinion, must guide an individual's actions.

Emerson, Thoreau and Rose soon confronted an issue that would overshadow all others—the urgent necessity of abolishing slavery. Thoreau would refuse to pay his taxes and would serve time in jail as a protest against the government's position on slavery. "Under a government which imprisons any unjustly," he wrote, "the true place for a just man is also a prison . . . [Prison] is the only house in a slave state in which a free man can abide with honor."[35] Later in 1844, Emerson would deliver a powerful speech condemning slavery, "Emancipation in the British West Indies."[36] Ernestine Rose would soon travel to the South and witness slavery, an experience that would transform her into an ardent abolitionist.

Rose's Amory Hall lectures caught the attention of a freethought newspaper, the *Boston Investigator*. This paper described her oratorical skills in an article, "Mrs. Rose, Social Lecturer":

> Within the past week, this highly accomplished lady . . . has delivered several lectures in this city . . . on the interesting subject of Social Reform . . . She lectured . . . on Sunday forenoon and evening in Amory Hall . . . Nothing could more forcibly mark the interest and attention of the audiences, than the excellent order preserved during her lectures, which were often nearly two hours long . . .
>
> Mrs. Rose has extraordinary powers to enchain the minds of an audience. Her personal appearance wins the attention and respect of her hearers, the moment she rises. Her head is marked with traits of high intellectual dignity. The lines of her countenance express gravity and deep thought mingled with much gentleness, and the beautifully expanded forehead towers above them, a fit abode for the lofty intellect dwelling therein. Her eye[s] [are] large and beaming, and in moments of inspiration, dilate with wonderful lustre [sic]. Her voice is very pleasant—full, rich and varied; and her gestures singularly graceful, expressive and appropriate.[37]

The attention given to Rose's appearance in this article attests to the rarity of female public speakers in the 1840's. Rose stood out, in addition, because she did not cover her hair, unlike two Quaker abolitionists, Angelina and Sarah Grimké, who spoke publicly in the 1830's.

Ernestine Rose was lecturing on women's rights at about the same time as another learned woman, Margaret Fuller, born in the same year as Rose, who led a series of "Conversations" for women in Boston. In these talks, she encouraged women to be more self-reliant and to develop their full potential for the benefit of themselves and for society. Fuller published her well-known book, *Woman in the Nineteenth Century* on this theme in 1845. In it she wrote, "We would have every path laid open to Woman as freely as to Man . . . Let them be sea-captains, if you will." She left the United States for Italy in 1846, becoming the first American woman to work as a foreign journalist. Fuller published articles on the Italian Revolution of 1848 before perishing in a shipwreck on her return trip to America in 1850.[38] Her tragic premature death prevented her from participating in the burgeoning women's rights movement. Fuller and Rose apparently never met.

Rose became an itinerant lecturer beginning in the 1840's. She traveled by train, horse-drawn coach or carriage from town to town at a time when traveling was slow and difficult. She visited most of the cities in New York and many in New Jersey, Connecticut, Massachusetts, Pennsylvania and Delaware. She traveled west to Ohio, visiting cities and "several settlements in the backwoods of Ohio" before traveling to Michigan and Indiana.

On her return home from a lecture tour in Indiana in 1845, Rose fell severely ill in Buffalo with "ague," a form of malaria. With symptoms of "brain fever," "delirium" and extreme weakness, she stayed with a Quaker family, the Howlands, who "spared neither attention nor expense to save her life and make her comfortable." Her husband traveled there to help nurse her back to health.[39] William Rose wrote to Robert Owen about his stay in Buffalo with his sick wife: "I arrived here on Friday morning and I found My Dear Ernestine was very low with the remittent Brain fever, but since then she has been better, and then worse again . . . She is very feeble and great care has to be taken with her . . . She is with very good and kind friends that do all they can for her."[40]

When Rose had recovered her health, she resumed traveling. She would visit twenty-three states in all. A journalist who interviewed her later remarked: "Some of these states she visited often, and on several occasions she addressed legislative bodies with marked effect . . . "[41] When she arrived at her destination, she did not always know where she would be housed, since she depended on her host or hostess to find lodging. During a trip she later took with her close friend, Susan B. Anthony, Anthony wrote that they were given "a little room not eleven feet square . . . The floor was strewn with papers, chips and straw—gave evidence of not having felt the impress of a broom for weeks."[42]

It was a grueling travel schedule, as described by her biographer, Jenny d'Héricourt:

> She would leave the train to speak for two or three hours on the rostrum, then climb aboard the train to do the same thing in other places. Often sick, unable to eat, she would give three speeches in one day, each one several hours long. One could see her going from city to city, getting petitions signed against laws whose injustice she succeeded in making people understand. At other times, she convened meetings and later conventions.[43]

How did she accomplish this? It was largely thanks to the support—emotional and financial—that she received from William Rose, "the husband whom she chose with her heart,"[44] who "gladly furnished her the means of making her extensive tours . . . and kept their household running."[45] Although she was frequently away on tours, traveling sometimes for months at a time, their marriage would remain strong. They were deeply devoted to each other. As an Owenite, William Rose fully supported her causes, particularly abolitionism, freethought and women's rights.

How did she pay for her travel expenses, since she did not charge for any of her lectures? While his wife was away on one of her numerous tours, William Rose managed their business successfully and ran their household. Ernestine Rose continued to manufacture cologne paper. The Roses apparently led a frugal life. When not traveling, d'Héricourt noted that "[she] saw few people and did not make social calls." Her biographer alluded to their egalitarian marriage, in which they shared household chores and saved expenses by not hiring servants: "She takes care, not only of housework, but takes great pleasure in her home, 'listening to her pot sing,' as the good-wives say. [She] does not look down upon the idea of cleaning her own house, of cooking, and she finds the time to help her excellent husband in his work."[46] Her wardrobe would likely have been small—like that of most middle-class men and women of her era—and she would have carried a small valise with a change of clothes. The few extant portraits of Rose show her wearing a simple black dress adorned with a lace collar.

Contemporary newspaper articles described Rose's magnetic presence on the lecture platform. The editor of the *Boston Investigator* wrote in 1846: "Since the retirement of Frances Wright . . . we have had no female (and we might add, no male) lecturer . . . who will compare with Ernestine L. Rose." After delivering several addresses to the House of Representatives in Detroit, Michigan in 1846, the Detroit Legislature passed resolutions pressing her to continue her lectures there: "The undersigned [express their] high gratification and pleasure, with which, in common with the citizens of Detroit generally, they have listened to the interesting and instructive lectures delivered . . . by Mrs. Rose and they wish to solicit a new lecture. . . . "[47] Ernestine Rose is credited with being the first person to broach the subject of women's suffrage in Michigan.[48]

The subjects of her lectures were quite broad. Among them were: "'The Science of Government,' 'Political Economy,' 'Equal Rights of Women,' 'Antagonisms in Society,' and the 'Wrongs of the Oppressed.'" The historian Morris U. Schappes wrote of her: "Men who came to taunt stayed to listen, admire and respect."[49] Her colleague Paulina Wright Davis wrote that when Rose announced her lectures, they were often the subject of ridicule. No one could imagine a woman treating such subjects, and audiences were often initially hostile. Once they heard her, though, they admired "her clear, strong intellect, respected her logic, and many were her enthusiastic converts."[50]

Rose would later write to Susan B. Anthony about her decades of travel and lectures:

In spite of hardships, for it was not as easy to travel at that time as now, and the expense, as I never made a charge or took up a collection, I look back to that time, when a stranger and alone, I went from place to place, in highways and by-ways, did the work and paid my bills with great pleasure and satisfaction; for the cause gained ground, and in spite of my heresies I had always good audiences, attentive listeners and was well received wherever I went. . . . In 1847 and 1848, I spoke in Charleston and Columbia, in South Carolina.[51]

Her trips to the American South would soon bring her face to face with slavery. She would find herself in a hostile, threatening environment. Ernestine Rose could not have anticipated how much she would be changed by this encounter.

NOTES

1. Alexis de Tocqueville, *Democracy in America*, trans. Arthur Goldhammer (New York: Library of America, 2004[1835, 1840]), 3, 397, 400.

2. Edwin G. Burrows and Mike Wallace, *Gotham: A History of New York City to 1898* (New York: Oxford University Press, 1999), 469; Bonnie S. Anderson, *The Rabbi's Atheist Daughter: Ernestine Rose, International Feminist Pioneer* (New York: Oxford University Press, 2017), 46.

3. For more on plumbing in 19th century New York City, see Krystal d'Costa, "A Right to Be Clean: Sanitation and the Rise of New York City's Water Towers," February 18, 2013, https://www.blogs.scientificamerican.com/anthropology-in-practice/a-right-to-be-clean-sanitation-and-the-rise-of-new-york-citys-water-towers/.

4. "Broadway and Grand Street in 1830," The New York Public Library Digital Collections, https://www.digitalcollections.nypl.org/items/5e66b3e9-058d-d471-e040-e00a180654d7; "Broadway Between Howard and Grand Streets in 1840," The New York Public Library Digital Collections, https://www.digitalcollections.nypl.org/items/5e66b3e9-2034-d471-e040-e00a180654d7.

5. "New York," *The Liberator*, May 21, 1836; Carol A. Kolmerten, *The American Life of Ernestine L. Rose* (Syracuse: Syracuse University Press, 1999), 20–21.

6. Sean Wilentz, *Chants Democratic: New York City and the Rise of the American Working Class, 1788–1850* (New York: Oxford University Press, 1984), 286–287, 294.

7. Marilyn Richardson, ed., *Maria W. Stewart, America's First Black Woman Political Writer: Essays and Speeches* (Bloomington: Indiana University Press, 1987), 38.

8. Frances Wright's speaking career was cut short by domestic problems associated with her married life and pregnancies. See Kolmerten, 27–30.

9. Ernestine L. Rose, "Speech at the Tenth National Woman's Rights Convention, Cooper Institute," New York, May 10–11, 1860, in Stanton, Anthony, and Gage, eds., *History of Woman Suffrage*, vol.1: 692.

10. Ernestine L. Rose, "Speech at the New England Anti-Slavery Convention," May 30, 1860, in Paula Doress-Worters, ed., *Mistress of Herself: Speeches and Letters of Ernestine L. Rose, Early Women's Rights Leader* (New York: The Feminist Press, 2008), 188–189.

11. Ernestine L. Rose, quoted in Elizabeth Cady Stanton, Susan B. Anthony, Matilda Joslyn Gage, eds., *History of Woman Suffrage*, vol. 1: 693, Gutenberg E-book.

12. Ernestine L. Rose, "Letter to the Editor with Text of the New York State Married Women's Property Act," March 28, 1860, New York, in Doress-Worters, 258–259.

13. Doress-Worters, 258–259.

14. Philip Hone, *Diary* (1828–1851), ed. Bayard Tuckerman, vol. 1: June 2, 1836 (New York: Dodd, Mead and Company, 1889), https://archive.org.

15. Thomas Herttell (1771–1849) was a New York magistrate and legislator who advocated for women's rights and who opposed imprisonment for debt.

16. Kolmerten, 33.

17. Ernestine L. Rose, quoted in Stanton, Anthony, and Gage, eds., *History of Woman Suffrage*, vol. 1:100.

18. Doress-Worters, 10.

19. Ernestine L. Rose, "Letter to the Editor with Text of the New York State Married Women's Property Act," in Doress-Worters, 258–259.

20. Gilbert Vale, Editor of the *Beacon,* described Rose's speech in this newspaper on December 23, 1837; cited in Kolmerten, 35.

21. "Mrs. Ernestine L. Rose," *The Liberator*, May 16, 1856, reprinted from an article by L. E. Barnard, "Mrs. Ernestine L. Rose," in *The Excelsior.*

22. Thomas A. Edison, "The Philosophy of Thomas Paine," Thomas Paine Friends, Inc., https://www.thomas-paine-friends.org/edison-thomas_essay-on-paine.htm, 1–4.

23. Anderson, 54.

24. "Celebration of Paine's Birthday in New York," *Boston Investigator,* February 19, 1840, in Doress-Worters, 59–61.

25. Paula Doress-Worters, ed., "Madame Rose: A Life of Ernestine L. Rose as told to Jenny P. d'Héricourt," *Journal of Women's History* 15, no. 1 (Spring 2003): 9.

26. Ernestine L. Rose, "Letter to Robert Owen," December 1844, in Doress-Worters, ed., *Mistress of Herself*, 66.

27. L. E. Barnard, "Ernestine L. Rose," in Stanton, Anthony, and Gage, eds., *History of Woman Suffrage*, vol. 1: 98.

28. Ralph Waldo Emerson, *Selected Writings*, ed. William H. Gilman (New York: Signet Classics, 2003), ix–x.

29. Linck C. Johnson, "Reforming the Reformers: Emerson, Thoreau, and the Sunday Lectures at Amory Hall, Boston," *ESQ* 37, 4th Quarter (1991): 237.

30. For more on Emerson's and Thoreau's lectures in 1844, see Johnson, 264, 275. Thoreau, then twenty-seven years old, would move to Walden Pond the following year.

31. Johnson, 241.

32. Ernestine L. Rose, speech cited in *Communitist,* October. 2, 1844, in Kolmerten, 49.

33. Ernestine L. Rose, "Speech at the Infidel Convention," May 4, 1845, cited in Doress-Worters, ed., *Mistress of Herself*, 69–70.

34. Wilentz, 302, 305.

35. Henry David Thoreau, "Civil Disobedience," in *The Writings of Henry David Thoreau*, ed. Horace Elisha Scudder et al.,vol. 10:149 (Boston: Houghton Mifflin Company, 1893).

36. Johnson, 279.

37. "Mrs. Rose, Social Lecturer," *Boston Investigator*, March 27, 1844.

38. Margaret Fuller, *Woman in the Nineteenth Century* (New York: Greeley & Mc Elrath, 1845), 26.

39. Paulina W. Davis, *A History of the National Woman's Rights Movement* (Reprint, New York: Source Books, 1970 [1871]), 11, cited in Anderson, 185.

40. William E. Rose, "Letter to Robert Owen," Sept. 31 [sic], 1845, in Doress-Worters, ed., *Mistress of Herself*, 71.

41. "Ernestine L. Rose," in Stanton, Anthony, and Gage, eds., *History of Woman Suffrage*, vol. 1: 98–99; Barnard, "Mrs. Ernestine L. Rose," *The Liberator*, May 16, 1856.

42. Susan. B. Anthony Diary, in *Selected Papers of Elizabeth Cady Stanton and Susan B. Anthony*, vol. 1: 294–295 (New Brunswick: Rutgers University Press, 1997).

43. Doress-Worters, ed.,"Madame Rose," 7.

44. "Madame Rose," 9.

45. "Ernestine L. Rose," in Stanton, Anthony, and Gage, eds., *History of Woman Suffrage*, vol. 1: 98.

46. "Madame Rose," 9.

47. "Mrs. Ernestine L. Rose," *Boston Investigator*, July 29, 1846, 1.

48. "Ernestine L. Rose" in Stanton, Anthony, and Gage, eds., *History of Woman Suffrage*, vol. 3: 514.

49. Morris U. Schappes, "To Be Included," *Morning Freiheit*, March 13, 1948.

50. Paulina W. Davis, quoted in Anderson, 184–185.

51. Ernestine L. Rose, "Letter to Susan B. Anthony," January 9, 1877, in Stanton, Anthony, and Gage, eds., *History of Woman Suffrage,* vol.1: 99.

Chapter 3

Confronting Slavery and Racism

In the years since their arrival in America, the Roses' adopted country was becoming ever more deeply divided over slavery. Slavery made the nation "a traitor to its great idea—that all men are born equal, each with the same inalienable rights."[1] The antislavery movement gained momentum in the 1830's and 1840's under the leadership of William Lloyd Garrison, who argued, through his widely-read newspaper, *The Liberator,* for an immediate and complete emancipation of slaves, a boycotting of slave products and a repudiation of unjust laws. Garrison was a radical Christian abolitionist and pacifist who denounced the Constitution and American political system, believing that they were corrupted by slavery. His pacifism allowed him few tactical options for ending slavery, however, other than nonviolent resistance.

The Grimké sisters, Sarah and Angelina, who were the first female abolitionists in America, organized a national women's antislavery convention in 1837 that attracted many activists, including Lucretia Mott, Maria Chapman, Lydia Maria Child and Abby Kelley.

Frederick Douglass escaped from slavery in 1838, taught himself to read and write, and founded an antislavery newspaper, the *North Star.*[2] By the 1840's, Douglass had become the nation's best known antislavery orator and activist. His autobiography, *Narrative of the Life of Frederick Douglass, an American Slave,* followed by two later autobiographical works, became best-sellers and played a major role in promoting the cause of abolition.

As the struggle for emancipation gained wider support, opposition to the antislavery movement grew more violent. Elijah Lovejoy, a young antislavery minister and newspaper editor, was murdered by a mob in 1837 as he was defending his printing press in Alton, Illinois. One year later, a mob in Philadelphia set fire to the building where a women's antislavery convention had been meeting, burning the building down.[3]

The atmosphere in Washington, D.C. became increasingly charged as the chasm between the North and South and between proslavery and antislavery factions widened, year by year. Following the annexation of Texas and the

Mexican-American War of 1846–1848, there was a political firestorm over the question of whether slavery could expand throughout the country. With the nation's acquisition of a million square miles of new territory, abolitionists saw this war as an attempt by slave states to extend slavery into the newly acquired land. Philip Hone, a wealthy merchant and former New York mayor, wrote in his diary in February 1850: "The dissolution of the Union, which until now it was treason to think of, much more to utter, is the subject of the daily harangues in both Houses of Congress. Compromise is at an end."[4]

Under pressure from Southern politicians, Congress passed the Fugitive Slave Act in September 1850, which required citizens and local governments to capture runaway slaves and which denied fugitives a right to a jury trial. For those opposed to slavery, nothing exposed more harshly than this law the brutality and inhumanity of this institution.

The firestorm over slavery grew ever more intense. The Kansas-Nebraska Act of 1854 led directly to armed conflicts, as it let citizens in these territories applying for statehood decide whether or not their state would allow slavery. This act overturned the Missouri Compromise of 1820. It was the Kansas-Nebraska Act that would cause forty-five-year-old Abraham Lincoln to re-enter politics, leaving his law practice after he had served two years in the House of Representatives.[5]

Lincoln could not contain his anger when the Supreme Court ruled in 1857 that Dred Scott, an enslaved person living in a free state, was not entitled to freedom because as a Black person he was not a citizen. Lincoln denounced the decision as a "slander and profanation" upon the Founders. The Dred Scott ruling covered over slavery, "the sum of all villainies," wrote Lincoln, with the "deceitful cloak" of self-government in an effort to conceal the "hateful carcass" beneath.[6]

Ernestine Rose had been speaking out against racism and slavery as early as the 1830's when she joined Robert Owen's association in England. "Twenty years ago I presided over an association for the protection of human rights, which embraced all colors, and nations, and sects," she told listeners, "and I stand on the same platform still." She would continue to denounce slavery and racism for the next three decades in the United States.[7]

Rose's ideology regarding human rights can be summed up succinctly: all human beings possess inalienable rights as members of the species; all have the potential for self-awareness and for greatness when they are free from social and cultural constraints. "Humanity's children are, in my estimation, all one and the same family," Rose asserted, "inheriting the same earth; therefore there should be no slaves of any kind among them."[8]

Rose was one of the rare social reformers of her era to give antislavery speeches in the American South and border states, where she traveled at great personal risk in 1847 and 1854.[9] Proslavery advocates often violently attacked those who criticized the institution of slavery. Rose's antislavery speeches from the 1840's have not been preserved but newspaper articles mention her appearances at rallies. The *New York Anti-Slavery Standard* of September 5, 1849, in an article about her speech at a West Indian Emancipation rally, noted: "Mrs. Rose . . . the eloquent Pole, showed that she has a vein of kindness and charity running through her every look, thought and word . . . She views humanity as one great unity, and thus an injury to one is an injury to all . . . Consequently, all mankind are her brethren, and the meanest does not escape her attention."[10]

The *New York Tribune* of May 17, 1850 reported Rose's appearance, along with that of Frederick Douglass, William Lloyd Garrison and Wendell Phillips, at a rally of the American Anti-Slavery Society in New York. This is the first documented meeting of Douglass and Rose, who would speak on the same abolitionist and women's rights platforms together for decades. The *Tribune* reported that as abolitionists attempted to speak, they were shouted down by a mob yelling racist slurs and catcalls.

According to the *Tribune* reporter, the leader of a so-called "law and order" party attending the Anti-Slavery Society rally, Captain Rynders, led diabolical shouts of "Douglass! Douglass!" "We want to hear a nigger!" "Mrs. Rose!" "Where's that sweet rose?" "Women's rights, boys!" "Oh, hell! Let's go and drink!" Catcalls and jeers ensued. A voice called out: "Have some respect for the ladies," to which Rynders retorted: "I have always respected the presence of ladies but I doubt very much whether white women who cohabit and mix with the woolly-headed negro are entitled to any respect from a white man." The reporter described Mrs. Rose, "all the time standing in the pulpit, looking like patience on a monument. At length she [Rose] said: 'Are you done? My friends, you have had your say out.'"[11] Finding that she could not be heard through the shouting, Rose finally left the stage. Policemen at the rally were unable—or perhaps unwilling—to stop the bedlam.

The abolitionists' futile efforts to calm the agitated crowd at the New York Anti-Slavery Society rally attest to the upheaval and mayhem in America. Rowdy gangs and ruffians attended antislavery rallies in order to disrupt them and to intimidate speakers. Even worse, as in Philadelphia, mobs might set fire to a building where an antislavery convention was held.

Rose continued her activism as an abolitionist, traveling throughout the Northeast. She gave an antislavery speech on August 4, 1853, at the celebration of "West Indian Emancipation," the antislavery movement's equivalent of American Independence Day, commemorating the British emancipation of enslaved people in Caribbean colonies. She brought to this speech her international perspective: Great Britain had abolished slavery in its colonies in 1833, while America, with its famed freedom, had not done this. She challenged America to live up to its principles.

At the picnic and meeting held that summer day, several hundred Black and white men and women braved the unsettled weather to enjoy lunch at a pleasant grove in Flushing, Queens. The crowd grew to five or six hundred by 1 pm and just as speeches were about to begin, a sudden shower forced the listeners to take shelter in a large barn, where they crowded together to listen to the addresses. The celebration and lectures would continue until 5:30 in the afternoon and would conclude with a collection of funds for an abolitionist pamphlet. A Black minister, Reverend Tunis Campbell, who often accompanied Frederick Douglass at antislavery meetings, offered a prayer for the abolition of slavery. A Black choir sang hymns, accompanied by the audience. William Lloyd Garrison then gave an address, followed by Ernestine Rose. Both would speak for a long time.

Public speaking was an art form and an important social and political event appreciated by large audiences. Great orators like Ernestine Rose spoke without notes, often relating humorous personal anecdotes and inviting audience response. The chair introduced Rose as "a speaker from that portion of mankind who are not always represented on occasions like this by their own orators."[12] She stood out as the only Jewish, immigrant speaker and the only woman at this event.

Rose began by speaking of the tradition of celebrating American anniversaries such as the Pilgrim Fathers' landing and Independence Day. She identified with her listeners, saying that while she was not American by birth, "My heart is always with those who do [celebrate], for they hail a day of freedom." July 4th was, in Rose's opinion, "that great and glorious day [which] gave to the world a great truth—that all men are born free and equal, and are therefore entitled to life, liberty, and the pursuit of happiness."

Abruptly, Rose changed her tone to point out a cruel irony: "Ah! Were only that great noble truth of the Declaration of Independence carried out, as it ought to be, there would be no need of our meeting here today." The audience broke into applause as Rose said that while Americans had waged war against England to create a democracy, it was England that had emancipated its slaves, while America failed to live up to its lofty ideals:

> In comparison to the liberation of 800,000 slaves, the Declaration of Independence falls into utter insignificance. It falls short, just as theory falls short of practice. There is an almost immeasurable distance between the two. The one was the utterance of a great truth that will last forever; the other was a practical application of it . . . The Declaration of Independence—has it yet abolished Slavery? But the great act of emancipation of 800,000 human beings has shown to the world that the African race are not only capable of taking care of themselves, but are capable of enjoying peacefully as much liberty and as much freedom as the white men.

Rose, attacking racist attitudes towards Blacks, anticipated the message of the American civil rights movement a century later.

As Rose spoke of slavery, she shifted from the first-person singular form, "I" to its plural form, "we," and then to the second person, "you" as she personalized this experience to her audience, asking listeners to not just think about it but to feel it as well:

> It is utterly impossible for us, as finite beings, with the utmost stretch of the imagination, to conceive the depth and immensity of the horrors of slavery. I would that, instead of speaking and listening today, we could all sit down in perfect silence and each and every one of us ask ourselves what is it to be a slave? . . . We have the evil among us; we see it daily and hourly before us . . . but do we comprehend it—do we realize it—do we feel it? What is it to be a slave? Not to be your own, bodily, mentally or morally—that is to be a slave. . . . To work hard, to fare ill, to suffer hardship, that is not slavery . . . Slavery is, not to belong to yourself—to be robbed of yourself. There is nothing that I so much abhor as that single thing—to be robbed of one's self. . . .
>
> Nature has not created masters and slaves; nature has created man as free as the air of heaven. The black man and the white man are equally the children of nature. The same mother earth has created us all; the same life pervades all; the same spirit ought to animate all. Slavery deprives us of ourselves. The slave has no power to say, 'I will go here, or I will go yonder.' The slave cannot say, 'My wife, my husband, or my child.' He does not belong to himself, and of course cannot claim anything whatever as his own. This is the great abomination of slavery: that it deprives a man of the common rights of humanity, stamped upon him by his Maker.[13]

Rose depicted the cruelty of slavery in powerful rhetoric as she switched to the pronoun "we" and then to the second-person pronouns, "you," "yourself." She was asking listeners to experience something that most people can scarcely comprehend because of its horrors. Rose had witnessed slavery firsthand, as she would soon relate. As a rationalist, Rose described slavery as violating natural laws by denying the equality of human beings. For a person who rejected religion, she chose surprisingly religious language by saying that slavery violated the sanctity of each person's "humanity, stamped upon him by his Maker" and that "the same spirit ought to animate all life." She chose these words because of their deep emotional appeal to her audience. Perhaps unconsciously she was reverting to expressions and precepts she had absorbed from her Jewish upbringing.

The power of Rose's words reminds us of one of Frederick Douglass's most stirring addresses on slavery, which he gave on July 5, 1852: his "Fourth of July" speech:

What, to the American slave, is your 4th of July? I answer; a day that reveals
to him, more than all other days in the year, the gross injustice and cruelty to
which he is the constant victim. To him, your celebration is a sham; your boasted
liberty, an unholy license; your national greatness, swelling vanity; your sounds
of rejoicing are empty and heartless; your denunciation of tyrants, brass fronted
impudence; your shouts of liberty and equality, hollow mockery.[14]

Douglass heightened the sense of isolation and betrayal felt by Blacks,
whom he distanced from his white listeners when he spoke of "your" 4th
of July. He had told his audience earlier in the speech, "*You* may rejoice; I
must mourn." Rose, like Douglass, addressed her listeners personally in the
second-person form to stir their feelings of empathy for slaves' suffering.
Both stressed the theme of America's unfulfilled promises of equality and
freedom. Since Rose and Douglass spoke together on the same antislavery
platforms and knew each other well, it is not surprising that some of their
speeches echoed one another.

Lightening the mood, Rose noted that since she was not a native of this
country, she probably had different ideas from other abolitionists. "I do
not belong to any abolition society, as my friend by my side [referring to
Garrison] said he was compelled to belong to the Garrisonian Society . . ."
Rose was proclaiming her independence while gently mocking her friend
Garrison for feeling "compelled" to belong to a society whose goal was liberation. She continued: "I go for emancipation of all kinds—white and black,
man and woman. Humanity's children are, in my estimation, all one and the
same family, inheriting the same earth; therefore there should be no slaves of
any kind among them. There are ties that bind man to man far stronger than
the ties of nation . . . and these are the ties of humanity." Martin Luther King,
Jr., in his powerful oratory over a century later, would echo Rose's words.

Shifting to anecdotal narrative, Rose talked about her 1847 trip to the South
in a lighthearted way, relating how she had met a lawyer who said that the
South could dissolve the Union because they didn't need or want the North.
"I let him go on for some time," Rose said, "for I knew he would run himself
out (Laughter interrupts her.) . . . I told him, 'I did not wish to have the Union
dissolved; I would like to stick to you, because you need us . . . Who are your
teachers and professors? Northern men. Who weaves your cloth and bedecks
you? Northern laborers. Who grows much of the food that nourishes you?
Northern men. Indeed, so greatly impoverished is the land in the South that it
is a positive fact, that I once saw a cow held up while she was fed.'"

After laughter had subsided, Rose made an appeal to boycott slave products, reasoning that "not being able to find a market for their products, slaveholders would have to either go to work to feed their slaves or free them." She
continued her narrative: "When I first stepped on slave soil, I read the curse of

Slavery upon it . . . I told [a gentleman in South Carolina], 'I'm sorry to say that you're a century, at least, behind us in the means of civilization . . . The slaves are the only civilized ones among you, because they do all the work.'"

Rose kept listeners entranced by her shifting between comedic and somber tones. In a similar way, Lincoln was known to interject humorous personal anecdotes into many of his speeches.

She then related the Southern lawyer's growing anger:

[The lawyer] You should thank your stars for being a woman.

[Rose] I always thanked my stars for being a woman, but I'd like to know [why I should] thank my stars in this particular instance.

[The lawyer] Our State has made a provision for many cases . . . For instance— when we catch a good Abolitionist, we give him a coat of tar and feathers.

[Rose] As for me, I'm an abolitionist in the fullest sense of the word and you are so exceedingly lazy and inactive here that it would be an act of charity to give you something to do, were it even to give me a coat of tar and feathers.

"To say that he was enraged would express no idea whatever," Rose continued, amid laughter and applause. She then repeated the defiant words she had spoken to the startled lawyer: "My dear sir, you have to thank yourself for this altercation; I did not begin it . . . You thought I would be a coward and recreant to my sentiments. I tell you sir, that if I had never been an abolitionist before, I would have become one here and you would have helped to make me one."

As Rose did in many of her speeches, she broadened the themes of racism and oppression to include all human rights: "The same rights to life and liberty that pertain to men pertain to women as well." To resounding applause, she concluded her address: "Emancipation from every kind of bondage is my principle. I go for the recognition of human rights, without distinction of sect, party, sex or color."[15]

How did Ernestine Rose avoid being physically attacked in South Carolina? The angry lawyer may have been overcome with astonishment at an outspoken woman like Rose, since antislavery orators and in particular female abolitionists so rarely came to the Deep South. According to her friend Moncure D. Conway, a Unitarian minister, "It was partly due to her sex, and partly to the paralysis caused by her audacity, that she was not torn to pieces; as it was, it required considerable influence to get her safely out of the city."[16]

In March and early April of 1854, Rose traveled with her close friend and fellow reformer, Susan B. Anthony, to Washington, D.C., to Virginia and the border state of Maryland, on a lecture tour that they hoped would "exercise a moral influence over Congress" to pass women's rights legislation.[17]

Anthony, born into a Quaker family in Adams, Massachusetts, was ten years younger than Rose and was the trip's organizer while Rose, as an experienced orator, gave all the public addresses. Anthony had become a schoolteacher and had been active in the temperance movement, which offered women a chance to speak in public about social ills. She had recently become involved in abolitionist and women's rights causes, but Anthony did not speak much in public until she and Elizabeth Cady Stanton became good friends and co-workers, soon after Anthony's trip with Rose.[18]

To an onlooker, the two women must have appeared very different. Anthony wore her brown hair tightly pulled back in a bun in the Quaker style; she was methodical and highly efficient as a trip planner. Rose, on the other hand, looked more exotic with her loose, curly hair. She was more spontaneous and carried no notes with her. The trip demanded great courage from both women since Rose was planning to address the subject of slavery in a proslavery region while also planning to speak about women's rights. The proposed Kansas-Nebraska Act was a burning topic, sparking debate in Congress and in many newspaper editorials. It was creating a highly charged atmosphere in Washington, D.C.

Visitors who came to the nation's capital in 1854 described the Mall as a "cow pasture." The Washington Monument and the Capitol building were both under construction. Two wings were being added to the Capitol and its dome enlarged. Nearby streets were overrun with geese, chicken, pigs and cows.[19] Susan B. Anthony kept a diary of her trip with Ernestine Rose and recorded their impressions of the region as well as of individuals they encountered:

> March 29. Mt. Vernon [Virginia] . . . The location of Washington's home is most beautiful and commanding, but, oh, the air of dilapidation and decay that everywhere meets the eye, the tottering out-buildings, the mark of slavery o'ershadow[ing] the whole . . . It would seem that, if the profession of reverence for the 'Father of his Country' were real, that this home of Washington would be rescued from the curse of slave labor, and made to blossom in the sunshine of free labor.[20]

Anthony was struck by the irony that both the nation's capital and the home of the "Father of his Country, George Washington," important symbols of democracy, were defiled by slavery.

It was during their overnight stay in a boarding house in Baltimore, Maryland, that the two women came face to face with slavery. Anthony recorded in her diary:

> April 2. A little colored boy came into our room with Sarah, the Chambermaid.

Mrs. Rose asked:

> Whose boy is that, Sarah?
> He belongs to Mrs. Waters, Miss.
> Where is his mother?
> She is Cook in the kitchen, Miss.
> Where is his Father?
> On the Eastern Shore, Miss.
> Is he a slave?
> Yes, Miss.
> Does he come to see his wife?
> No, Miss, not since my mistress moved to the City.
> Has Cook any more children?
> Yes, Miss, two more little boys younger than this.

Oh, how did my blood run chill.

Anthony noted in her diary her conversation with Sarah and her reaction afterwards:

> Are you free, Sarah?
> No, Miss.
> Do you belong to Mrs. Waters?
> No, Miss, she hires me of my Master for $8 per month.
> And don't you get any portion of it?
> No, Miss, only my Master gives me my clothes.
> Does he keep you well clothed?
> Sometimes, Miss, and sometimes I gets [sic] short.
> And don't you have any pocket money of your own?
> Yes, Miss, what the ladies gives [sic] me.

> . . . Oh how I long to probe her soul in search of the Divine spark that scorns to be a slave. But then would it be right for me by so doing to add to the burden of her wretched life? [21]

Both Rose and Anthony would become passionate abolitionists after seeing firsthand the destructive and dehumanizing effects of slavery on families.

Anthony and Rose were unable to reserve a hall for Rose's speech in the Capitol building, because the Speaker of the House told them that he could not allow a person "who failed to recognize the Divine, to speak in his place . . . " Anthony wrote in her diary: "I remarked to him that ours was a country professing Religious as well as Civil Liberty and not to allow any and every faith to be declared in the Capitol . . . made the profession of religious freedom a perfect mockery."[22]

Rose lectured on women's rights at Carusi's Saloon, an assembly hall in Washington, D.C., in Alexandria, Virginia and in Baltimore. "[Rose's] meetings have all been but thinly attended, compared with our Northern meetings," wrote Anthony. "Still, the people here call the audiences large . . . Few people here seem to be in the least interested in any subject of reform. The only thing that in any way alarms them is the fear that some word shall be uttered which shall endanger their 'pet institution' [slavery]."

Anthony must have frightened the proprietor of a hall when she told him bluntly: " . . . I wish you to understand that Mrs. Rose is an out and out abolitionist. She is here to speak on women's rights . . . but if she should feel disposed, as I hope she will, to give an antislavery lecture, she will inform all parties of her intentions."[23] Rose would be "breaking up the time-hardened soil" and "agitating" in a region not yet open to reform.

Rose gave a lecture titled, "The Nebraska Question, as Deduced from Human Rights," at Carusi's Saloon, a speech which she later described as a turning point in her views on the abolition of slavery. She would say in 1855: "Last March . . . I spoke on the Nebraska Bill. When I went to the lecture room, I had no idea that I was a Disunionist; I never knew it; I never suspected it. But while there . . . I endeavored to find some reasons to show why the Union need not be dissolved, and yet slavery be abolished—for I had been antislavery all my lifetime . . . I convinced myself of the impossibility of it, and I said so at the time. . . . and when I went home from that lecture, I said to a friend of mine, 'If I have not succeeded in convincing anyone else, I have succeeded—and am very happy to know it—in convincing myself.'"[24]

Her firsthand confrontation with slavery had made her rethink her views. Rose felt that separating the North from the South—"disunion" or secession—was preferable to accepting compromises such as the Nebraska Bill in order to placate proslavery states and keep the union together. Rose's views were evolving. She had become more radicalized while speaking about the Nebraska question.

Although her speech on the Nebraska Question was not recorded, a journalist in the *Washington Globe* wrote a review of it. He praised her for "treating the subject in a truly masterly manner," but then went on to misrepresent her ideas by ascribing to Rose the arguments of the South; namely, that the South could not be expected to relinquish its slaves because "Slavery had been handed down to [them] . . . " Rose published a letter to the editor a few days later to correct misinformation and to expand on her views on the Nebraska Bill:

> [I believe] man has an inalienable right to himself . . . and no reason or argument has a feather weight in the balance against Human Freedom. Yet I can have pity . . . for the slaveholder . . . It is an eternal law of humanity that the wrongdoer shall suffer from the evils he perpetrates on others.

But the men of the North . . . who profess free principles . . . what can we say to such if they pander to the slave principles of the South? . . . I am compelled to feel utter contempt for Northern men, who simply, for the sake of office, introduce and support the Nebraska Bill.[25]

Rose's trips to the Deep South and to the proslavery border states had now convinced her that "disunion" was inevitable in order to save American democracy.

During their travels together, Rose confided in her friend Susan B. Anthony that two antislavery advocates, Lucy Stone and Wendell Phillips, had expressed anti-Semitic views and prejudice against giving foreigners the rights of citizenship. Anthony's diary notes showed the extent of Rose's isolation as an immigrant, freethinker and Jew within the reform movements of her day. Anthony recorded her painful exchange with Rose:

I said, 'Mrs. Rose, there is not *one* in the Reform ranks, whom you think true, not *one* but who panders to the popular feeling?'
[Rose] said, 'I can't help it. I take them by the words of their own mouths. I trust all until their words or acts declare them false to truth and right,' and, continued she, 'no one can tell the hours of anguish I have suffered, as one after another I have seen those whom I had trusted betray falsity of motive as I have been compelled to place one after another on the list of panderers to public favor.'[26]

Anthony tried to console her friend by offering her poetry, but inadvertently made her pain even greater by giving her a verse from a Christian hymn. She was unintentionally reminding Rose of her outsider status as a non-Christian and nonbeliever. The two friends wept together. Rose's despairing words, "I expect never to be understood while I live," brought tears to Anthony's eyes and led her to write prophetically in her diary: "Mrs. Rose is not appreciated nor cannot be by this age. She is too much in advance of the extreme ultraists even, to be understood by them."[27]

Rose denounced the prejudices of those who claimed to hold progressive, liberal views as abolitionists and women's rights activists. Lucy Stone and Wendell Phillips revealed their biases in letters and speeches. In one letter Stone sent to Anthony, she severely criticized Rose, saying that although she "spoke well" at a convention, "there are so many mean Jews" there "and her face is so essentially Jewish, that people remarked the likeness and feared her."[28] Wendell Phillips, quoted in the *New York Times*, said at a women's rights convention: "The movement for woman's rights was an instinctive effort on the part of half the race—the genuine Saxon race—for elbow room. . . . "[29] Despite Phillips' courageous activism, his bigoted characterization of the women's movement excluded a large number of Americans, including Blacks and Jews.

Ernestine Rose continued to speak out against slavery in many different settings, inspired by personal testimonies she had heard from enslaved or formerly enslaved people during her lecture tours. Her extensive travels undermined her health, though. After she returned from her springtime tour with Anthony, she developed an "inflammation of the lungs," which prevented her from participating in women's rights conventions that summer.[30]

She resumed her lecture tours in the fall and by 1855, her most prolific year, she had become one of the most famous female lecturers in the United States. Lemuel E. Barnard, a journalist, wrote of her: "As an advocate of women's rights, antislavery and religious liberty, Rose has earned a world-wide celebrity."[31]

When Rose spoke at the New England Anti-Slavery Convention on May 29, 1855, she was accompanied by Reverend Thomas Wentworth Higginson, a Unitarian minister who had helped to liberate fugitive slaves. Higginson would later lead the 33rd Regiment, the first Black regiment in the Civil War, and would publish an account of his experiences.[32] Anthony Burns, a former slave whom Higginson had helped to liberate, gave his personal testimony in which he expressed his gratitude to be attending an antislavery convention—his first. He thanked all who had helped him. The audience would receive his concluding remarks with much feeling and applause:

> A year ago at this time, [I] was carried through the streets of Boston, a prisoner, and in the midst of troops, into the hell of Southern slavery. [I] did not then expect to be bought out of slavery, but [I] had the hope in [my] soul of seeing a free land again and of feeling the breath of the free air in Canada, at least in the course of two or three years. [I] am thankful to God that, whereas [I] was a chattel, now [I] am a man, or, if [I] am not yet [one], [I] hope to be.[33]

In her address at this convention, Rose began by speaking of the gap between America's professed values and the reality of its treatment of Blacks. She quoted an expression illustrating the wisdom of Quakers: "From monarchical and despotic countries we do not expect much; but those countries have a right to hold you to your professions. The Quakers say: 'According to the light you possess is the demand made upon you.' It is a true and correct saying. According to your professions, we have a right to hold you responsible; and therefore, this country stands responsible for its false and hypocritical professions without carrying out the great, eternal truth of the equality of man."

She personalized her remarks in a deeply emotional appeal to her audience, as she mentioned Anthony Burns:

I have heard many eloquent speeches from this platform, and from other anti-slavery platforms, but I was never so affected as I was this morning by the few simple words that fell from the lips of Anthony Burns. He stood here as a living, breathing, moving witness of the great iniquity of slavery. Only one year ago, he was doomed to slavery once more; and were it not that a few benevolent men were untiring and persistent in their determination to rescue him, cost what it would, Anthony Burns would not have been here this morning to give his evidence as he did, to the large audience that, slave as he was, crushed and oppressed as he was, chained, not only in body, but also in mind, nevertheless, he was a man; for there was the love of freedom and the determined purpose to achieve it whenever the opportunity was afforded.[34]

Rose went on to forcefully reject the racist views of many Americans, including those of scientists who offered pseudoscientific theories claiming that all races were not equal:

Even scientific men have come down from the glorious heights of science low enough to be bought by Southern gold and endeavor to prove that the colored man is a different being from the white man, and therefore it is right to hold him as a slave. . . . It is worse than time lost to enter into any such consideration . . . Humanity recognizes no color, mind recognizes no color; pleasure or pain, happiness or misery, life or death, recognizes no color . . . Like the white man, the colored man comes involuntarily into existence . . . Like him he ought to have all the rights and all the privileges that the country can bestow. Is that any more than any man ought to claim, and ought any man be satisfied with less?[35]

In her concluding comments, Rose affirmed beliefs she had expressed in her Nebraska Bill speech: "Disunion (separation of the North from the South) must come. There can be no union between freedom and slavery."[36]

Following the Dred Scott Supreme Court decision and the Kansas-Nebraska Act, many Northerners believed that the South was holding the nation hostage to demands that would make slavery national and permanent. When Lincoln ran for the Presidency in 1860 as an antislavery candidate in the Republican Party, he advocated a conservative position, remaining "steadfast to the principles of the [Founding] Fathers on the subject of slavery": namely, that the Constitution limited but did not attempt to destroy slavery where it already existed, since it considered it a dying institution.[37] Lincoln, an Enlightenment thinker, wanted to follow reason rather than passion, and see slavery ultimately abolished through laws.

Abolitionists such as Frederick Douglass and Ernestine Rose found Lincoln's conservative position morally unacceptable. Douglass felt that the Republican Party's reluctance to advocate for the abolition of slavery and its support for various forms of racial discrimination amounted to "treason against the slave and the Black man."[38] Both Douglass and Rose found it morally repugnant to agree to any compromise over the issue of slavery and both "agitated" through their speeches to move the nation towards emancipation. While Douglass espoused a branch of Christianity that believed that God commanded a violent overthrow of the slave system, Rose as a freethinker spoke of the natural inalienable rights to freedom and equality found in the Declaration of Independence.

Many of Rose's abolition speeches have been lost. The following excerpts are from a previously unpublished speech that she gave at the second anniversary of the founding of the Michigan Anti-Slavery Society on October 7, 1855. Rose appealed to her listeners' emotions and conscience as she evoked the horrors of slavery: "None but one who has been a slave and has the fire of freedom burning within him can truly represent slavery. Who can describe it—who can comprehend it? Slavery deprives the human being of his manhood, and deprived of that he is deprived of all. Make him believe he has no right to himself, and you cut off with him all right to claim anything that belongs to himself."

The evil of slavery, Rose continued, corrupted slaveholders and the entire South: "It is a law of right that the wrongdoer can never escape from the wrong he commits. The slaveholder is no exception. His children are left in the hands of the slaves and then receive a most unfavorable direction for a future character; hence the low standard of morality in the South. Industry is looked upon with contempt; look at the low standard of her civilization." Rose had observed during her travels in the South that slavery had created an impoverished land and one that tainted all who lived there, both children and adults.[39]

Rose then addressed the daunting challenge of how best to end slavery: "The question we have to settle is . . . the best means of doing away with this great evil." One solution she rejected was compromise to placate the South. She called on leaders instead to exert both economic and political pressures on the South: "Circumscribe and confine the Slave Power and it is doomed. Let the North raise the cry of *no slavery or no Union*. Let the political parties re-echo the cry. Some say the Constitution is an antislavery instrument. Then take it from the hands of the slaveholders." If these pressures failed to destroy slavery, then there would be no choice but to separate the North from the South: "As [for] the Union, there is none between the North and the South. I am not afraid of the dissolution of the alleged Union."

Rose asserted, dramatically: "As far as my power would go, I would use it for the power of human freedom. I go for the rights of women—of white women and Black women. There is no ground so sacred as that on which man stands. There is no question so sacred as man." She made a passionate, personal appeal to listeners to fight for the soul of the nation, concluding:

We are called upon to be living martyrs. To stand up among our fellow beings in defense of freedom when to do so compels us to a constant clashing with the opinions, prejudices and imagined interests of those around us—is a martyrdom far excelling that of those who lay down their heads on the block. You have done, you need covet no higher martyrdom. I hope all will labor for freedom; you will thus secure the highest reward, your own just approbation, and bring man back to himself.[40]

During the Civil War era, Rose was fighting two formidable battles—against slavery and racism. Susan B. Anthony wrote to Elizabeth Cady Stanton, "Mrs. Rose will come" to a series of meetings in New York. "[Rose] never felt so strong—to speak on Anti-Slavery."[41]

Rowdy crowds interrupted speeches and threatened violence. *The National Anti-Slavery Standard* of January 12, 1856 reported that ruffians in Bangor, Maine, threatened to attack Rose as she was preparing to give a talk, ironically, on "Human Rights and the Violation of Them." According to the reporter, "the proslavery sectarians . . . made a furious onset upon her, alleging that she was an infidel, and therefore unworthy to address a Christian assembly." The reporter observed what happened next:

[Despite their fuss] it was all of no avail. The managers . . . would not break an honorable engagement to gratify the spiteful bigotry of narrow-minded sectaries. Mrs. Rose appeared at the appointed time and delivered two lectures, making a highly favorable impression, and, by her womanly dignity and earnest devotion to the right, putting her enemies to shame.[42]

Despite rowdy crowds and ever-present threats of violence, the abolitionist cause was steadily gaining ground. More than a hundred members of Congress openly identified themselves as antislavery men by the late 1850's.[43]

On another occasion, at an antislavery rally in Albany, New York in February 1861, a mob threatened to disrupt the speeches but Mayor George Thatcher held his ground and brought in a police force to keep the peace. "Let at least the capital of the Empire State be kept free from the disgraceful proceedings which, in other localities, have brought dishonor upon our institutions," Mayor Thatcher said to the crowd. " . . . Come what may, mob law shall never prevail in our good city with my consent and connivance." Rose then delivered her abolitionist speech, saying that it was too late to send commissioners to meet with the South. "It is degradation! . . . Compromise now and within five years you will have a slave auction-block in front of your capitol . . . "[44]

In her 1861 speech at a Thomas Paine Celebration, just months before the outbreak of the Civil War, Rose proclaimed that the question facing the nation was no longer one of color. Instead, it was: "Shall henceforth freedom or slavery be the ruling principle of this republic? Freedom and slavery can-not live in harmony; the one must destroy the other . . . Whether the South is allowed to drift to her downward destiny, or forced into submission, let the watchword be, 'No more compromise!'"[45]

During the Civil War, Rose spoke out passionately about emancipation being the only acceptable moral reason for fighting the war. Without ending slavery, she believed, American democracy could not be saved. She criticized Lincoln for his handling of the war and for not emancipating slaves right way: "Let the Administration give evidence that they . . . are for justice to all, with-out exception, without distinction, and I, for one, had I ten thousand lives, would gladly lay them down to secure this boon of freedom to humanity!" Rose criticized General George McClellan for his incompetency, and Lincoln for not replacing him sooner: "Now, I say to Abraham Lincoln, if these gen-erals. . . . are good for nothing, dispose of them. . . . At all events, cut them loose from the pay . . . What has the great little Napoleon [a nickname for McClellan] done? Just enough to prevent anybody else from doing anything."

While Rose often spoke about peace, in this Civil War address she con-cluded by calling for strong military action as the only way to end slavery:

> This rebellion and this war have cost too dear. The money spent, the vast stores destroyed, the tears shed, the lives sacrificed, the hearts broken, are too high a price to be paid for the mere *name* of Union. I never believed we had a Union . . . I care not by what measure you end the war, if you allow one single germ, one single seed of slavery to remain in the soil of America . . . that nox-ious weed will thrive and again stifle the growth, wither the leaves, blast the flowers and poison the fair fruits of freedom . . . To avert such calamity, we must work. And our work must mainly be to watch and criticize and urge the Administration to do its whole duty to freedom and humanity.[46]

At an American Anti-Slavery Society Meeting in May 1862, a reporter noted that Rose "urged the publication in pamphlet form of a speech given by the abolitionist William Wells Brown." She offered to contribute money to help publish it. Brown, who had escaped from slavery, had spoken about the suc-cess of freed Blacks who supported themselves in the South. "One of the clearest demonstrations of the ability of the slave to provide for himself in a state of freedom," Brown had argued, "is to be found in the prosperous con-dition of the large free colored population of the Southern states. . . . " Their success had, however, exacerbated racial prejudice. Brown astutely observed: "It is this industry, this sobriety, this intelligence, and this wealth of the free colored people of the South that has created so much prejudice on the part of slaveholders against them."

The reporter remarked: "Rose considered [Brown's] speech the most important one of the day . . . and wished it . . . laid upon the desks of the members of Congress, and others, who may still be troubled with the absurd idea that the slaves, if set free, cannot take care of themselves." She offered a resolution in support of publishing his speech. William Wells Brown's speech was a premonition of the difficult path that lay ahead for Blacks, as systemic racism impeded the progress of freed slaves to forge an economically independent life in the United States. [47]

At a time when Frederick Douglass and Ernestine Rose were giving voice to bold ideas about racial equality, Lincoln was following a more conservative approach, adhering strictly to the letter of the law. Although he believed that slavery was immoral, President Lincoln wrote to the publisher Horace Greeley in August, 1862 during the Civil War: "My paramount object in this struggle *is* to save the Union and is *not* either to save or to destroy slavery. If I could save the Union without freeing any slave, I would do it, and if I could save it by freeing all of the slaves, I would do it, and if I could save it by freeing some and leaving others alone, I would do it."[48]

Lincoln's above words may seem surprising, considering the fact that he would issue the Emancipation Proclamation just five months later. As a wartime president, Lincoln was governing a nation deeply polarized over the slavery issue. Many congressmen from the Democratic Party, from both the Northern and border states, had proslavery and pro-Confederate leanings and might turn against the Union, making it impossible for him to effectively govern and to wage war.[49] In her criticism of Lincoln, Rose showed that she might not have understood the president's difficult political predicament.

Lincoln's issuing of the Emancipation Proclamation freed slaves in the Confederate states and allowed Blacks to enlist in the Union army. It still allowed slavery to continue, however, in the border states. Anti-war and anti-Republican sentiment grew and reached a boiling point in New York City in July 1863 as a result of a draft law that allowed wealthy men to either hire a substitute or pay $300 to be exempt from serving, while poor men had to serve. For four days, on July 13–16, mobs of angry white workers stormed federal and state buildings, pro-war newspaper offices, and homes of the wealthy. They set fires, looted and murdered individuals, turning their fury particularly on Blacks and overwhelming the city's police force. They attacked the Colored Orphan Asylum, setting it afire. Fortunately all the children were able to escape. At least 119 people were killed in the Draft Riots, one of the worst race-related riots in American history, before Union troops restored order in the city. Ernestine and William Rose, as residents in the Washington Square Park area, might have witnessed this terrible event.[50]

By 1864, Lincoln had become passionate about emancipation. He now believed that without the abolition of slavery, there could be no victory in the war.[51] When he later looked back, he would express his new understanding of its importance: "[Emancipation] is my greatest and most enduring contribution to the history of the war. It is, in fact, the central act of my administration, and the great event of the nineteenth century."[52]

While abolitionists spoke out for freedom and equality in America, soldiers of all races fought on battlefields, and an estimated 620,000 of them died during the Civil War in order to end slavery and save the Union. During the war, Ernestine Rose, Susan B. Anthony, Elizabeth Cady Stanton and other activists went door to door to collect signatures, ultimately gathering four hundred thousand signatures to demand the passage of the Thirteenth Amendment, which would prohibit slavery in the United States. When the bill fell thirteen votes short of the needed two-thirds majority in the House in 1864, Lincoln continued to press the House and to lobby senators from the border states. The Thirteenth Amendment at last passed on January 31, 1865. Members of Congress "fell silent . . . and wept like children" while outside, a hundred-gun salute announced the bill's passage.[53] Following the war, the federal government established the Freedmen's Bureau to provide food, clothing, and medical care to freed slaves and other refugees.[54]

The Reconstruction era would see the beginnings of multiracial democracy in America—an elusive goal that still remains unfulfilled. It would prove to be a difficult period for human rights activists. Congress raised their hopes and expectations when it passed in 1866 the first civil rights act in American history, defining citizenship by declaring: "All persons born in the United States and not subject to any foreign power, excluding Indians not taxed, are hereby declared to be citizens of the United States . . . All citizens have a right to equal protection under the law."[55] The political mobilization of Southern Blacks was a stunning achievement in 1867–1868—thousands of Blacks voted, contributing to the strength of the Republican Party in the South.[56]

Despite the civil rights act, the nation continued to deny equal rights to many, including women, Blacks, and other minorities. Frances Ellen Watkins Harper, a poet, abolitionist and suffragist, spoke of the plight of Blacks in 1866:

> Since the Dred Scott decision, I have sometimes said I thought the nation had touched bottom. But let me tell you there is a depth of infamy lower than that. It is when the nation, standing upon the threshold of a great peril, reached out its hands to a feebler race, and asked that race to help it, and when the peril was over, said, 'You are good enough for soldiers, but not good enough for citizens.'[57]

The Fourteenth and Fifteenth Amendments, in 1868 and 1870, respectively, "ensured" political equality to emancipated slaves. Southern states, nevertheless, were able to pass discriminatory acts known as Black Codes and Jim Crow laws that prevented Blacks from exercising their right to vote and that segregated them in all public places, while allowing the Ku Klux Klan to rampage across the country, threatening their lives.

Chinese Americans, both immigrants and citizens, faced discriminatory laws and racial violence, much like Blacks. The Chinese Exclusion Act of 1882 would prohibit all immigration of Chinese laborers and deny citizenship to those Chinese already living in the country.[58]

Ernestine Rose and Frederick Douglass were among a small group of social reformers of their era who had a vision of universal rights—a dream of all people enjoying equal rights in a nation made stronger not in spite of its diversity but because of it. Douglass made this argument in a speech he gave in Boston in 1869: "I want a home here not only for the Negro, the mulatto and the Latin races; but I want the Asiatic to find a home here in the United States, and feel at home here, both for his sake and for ours."[59] Rose did not advocate just for abolition, racial equality, women's rights and freethought, but for human rights—which encompassed them all. These causes were all of a piece for her. "I have faith, unbounded, unshaken faith in the principles of right, of justice, and humanity," she would proclaim.[60]

Frederick Douglass and Ernestine Rose did not exchange any letters that have survived, but Douglass wrote in his autobiography about Rose and other abolitionists who "met me as a brother, and by their kind consideration did much to make endurable the rebuffs I encountered elsewhere." Douglass mentioned abolitionists by name, including "the Roses. . . . and others whose names are lost, but whose deeds are living yet in the regenerated life of our new republic, cleansed from the curse and sin of slavery."[61]

NOTES

1. Theodore Parker, *A Sermon of Mexican War, Preached at the Melodeon*, June 7, 1846 (Boston: I.R. Butts, 1846), 32. Theodore Parker (1810–1860) was a Unitarian minister and abolitionist who would inspire Abraham Lincoln and Martin Luther King, Jr.

2. Philip S. Foner, ed., *Frederick Douglass on Women's Rights* (Westport: Greenwood Press, 1976), 8–12.

3. Carol A. Kolmerten, *The American Life of Ernestine L. Rose* (Syracuse: Syracuse University Press, 1999), 58–62.

4. Philip Hone, *Diary* (1828–1851), ed. Bayard Tuckerman, vol. 2: 884–885, February 18, 1850 (New York: Dodd, Mead and Company, 1889), https://archive.org. https://archive.org.

5. The Missouri Compromise admitted Missouri as a slave state but banned slavery in the remaining Louisiana Purchase lands north of the 36°30' parallel. See Jill

Lepore, *These Truths: a History of the United States* (New York: W.W. Norton, 2018), 179, 262–263.

6. Abraham Lincoln, in Roy P. Basler, ed., *The Collected Works of Abraham Lincoln* (New Brunswick: Rutgers University Press, 1953), vol. 2:454.

7. "Mrs. Rose's Lecture," *The Una* 2, no. 4 (April 1, 1854): 243.

8. Ernestine L. Rose, "Speech at the Anniversary of West Indian Emancipation," August 4, 1853, in Paula Doress-Worters, ed., *Mistress of Herself: Speeches and Letters of Ernestine L. Rose, Early Women's Rights Leader* (New York: The Feminist Press, 2008), 150.

9. The term "border states" during the Civil War era referred to proslavery states that did not secede from the Union. They included Delaware, Maryland, Kentucky, Missouri and West Virginia.

10. "Mrs. E. L. Rose," *New York Anti-Slavery Standard,* reprinted in the *Boston Investigator*, September 5, 1849, 3.

11. "American Anti-Slavery Society," *New York Tribune*, reprinted in *The Liberator*, May 17, 1850, 2.

12. Morris U. Schappes, "Ernestine L. Rose: Her Address on the Anniversary of West Indian Emancipation," *Journal of Negro History* 34, no. 3 (July 1949): 344–355. Schappes, an historian of Jewish history, rediscovered this address that had first appeared in *The National Anti-Slavery Standard* on August 13, 1853.

13. Ernestine L. Rose, "West Indian Emancipation Speech," in Doress-Worters, 147–152.

14. Frederick Douglass, "What to the Slave is the Fourth of July?" July 5,1852, https://www.democracynow.org/2021/7/5/james_earl_jones_frederick_douglass_july4.

15. Doress-Worters, 147–152.

16. Moncure D. Conway is quoted in Sara A. Underwood, "Ernestine L. Rose," *Heroines of Free Thought* (New York: C. P. Somerby, 1876), 271.

17. Ernestine Rose is quoted in the *New York Tribune*, October 10, 1853.

18. Barbara F. Berenson, *Massachusetts in the Woman Suffrage Movement*, (Charleston: The History Press, 2018), 40–41.

19. John W. Reps, *Washington on View: The Nation's Capital since 1790* (Chapel Hill: University of North Carolina Press, 1991), 112.

20. Susan B. Anthony, "Diary of Lecture Tour to the Border South with Ernestine L. Rose," March 24–April 14, 1854, in Doress-Worters, 170.

21. Doress-Worters, 171–172.

22. Doress-Worters, 170.

23. Susan B. Anthony, "Letter to the Editor, 'Slavery and Reform,'" *The Liberator*, April 14, 1854, quoted in Doress-Worters, 177.

24. Ernestine L. Rose, "Speech at the New England Antislavery Convention," May 30, 1855, in Doress-Worters, 192–193.

25. Ernestine L. Rose, "Letter to the Editor of the *Washington Globe*," March 31, 1854, in *The Una* 2, no. 5 (May 1854): 269–270.

26. Doress-Worters, 173.

27. Doress-Worters, 173.

28. Lucy Stone, Letter to Susan B. Anthony, November 2, 1855, in *Stanton and Anthony Papers*, microfilm, reel 8, frames 298–309, quoted in Bonnie S. Anderson, *The Rabbi's Atheist Daughter: Ernestine Rose, International Feminist Pioneer* (New York: Oxford University Press, 2017), 93.

29. Wendell Phillips, "Woman's Rights Convention in New York," cited in the *New York Times*, May 14, 1858, 5.

30. *Boston Investigator*, October 11, 1854, 3.

31. L.E. Barnard, "Mrs. Ernestine L. Rose," *The Liberator*, May 16, 1856.

32. For more on Thomas Wentworth Higginson as an abolitionist and soldier, see Doress-Worters, 187.

33. "New England Anti-Slavery Convention," *The Liberator* 25, no. 23 (June 8, 1855):1.

34. Ernestine L. Rose, "Speech at the New England Anti-Slavery Convention, May 30, 1855," in Doress-Worters, 187–189.

35. Doress-Worters, 190.

36. Doress-Worters, 193.

37. Lincoln, *Collected Works,* vol. 3: 552.

38. *Frederick Douglass Monthly*, August 1860, cited in James Oakes, *The Radical and the Republican: Frederick Douglass, Abraham Lincoln and the Triumph of Antislavery Politics* (New York: Norton, 2007), 130.

39. See Rose's "West Indian Emancipation Speech," in Doress-Worters, 150.

40. Ernestine L. Rose, "The Second Anniversary of the Michigan Anti-Slavery Society," in *The Anti-Slavery Bugle* 11, no. 11 (October 27, 1855):1.

41. Susan B. Anthony to Elizabeth Cady Stanton, December 23, 1860, in *The Selected Papers of Elizabeth Cady Stanton and Susan B. Anthony*, vol. 1: 452 (New Brunswick: Rutgers University Press, 1997).

42. "Pro-Slavery Bigotry Put to Shame," *The National Anti-Slavery Standard*, January 12, 1856.

43. Oakes, 88.

44. "The State Anti-Slavery Convention," in *The National Anti-Slavery Standard*, February 16, 1861 and February 23, 1861.

45. Ernestine L. Rose, "Speech at the Thomas Paine Celebration," January 29, 1861, in Doress-Worters, 292–294.

46. Ernestine L. Rose, "Speech at the National Convention of the Loyal Women of the Republic," May 14, 1863, in Doress-Worters, 306–307, 309–310.

47. "Twenty-Ninth Annual Meeting of the American Anti-Slavery Society," *The Liberator*, May 16, 1862, 3. William Wells Brown (1814 [?] –1884), like Frederick Douglass, was an eloquent antislavery orator and the author of several books, including a popular autobiography.

48. Abraham Lincoln, "Letter to Horace Greeley," August 1862, in *Collected Works*, vol. 5:388.

49. James M. McPherson, *Battle Cry of Freedom: The Civil War Era* (New York, Oxford University Press, 1988), 506–510.

50. Edwin G. Burrows and Mike Wallace, *Gotham: A History of New York City to 1898* (New York: Oxford University Press, 1999), 887–896.

51. McPherson, 503–504.

52. Abraham Lincoln is quoted in Allen C. Guelzo, "Emancipation and the Quest for Freedom," *The Civil War Remembered*, https://www.nps.gov/articles/ emancipation-and-the-quest-for-freedom.htm.

53. Lepore, 303–304.

54. "The Freedmen's Bureau," *National Archives*, https://www.archives.gov/ research/african-americans/freedmens-bureau.

55. Lepore, 319.

56. David W. Blight, *Race and Reunion: The Civil War in American Memory* (Cambridge: The Belknap Press of Harvard University, 2001), 47–49.

57. Frances Ellen Watkins Harper, "We Are All Bound up Together," Address given at the Eleventh National Women's Rights Convention in New York City in 1866, https://www.blackpast.org/african-american-history/speeches-african-american -history/1866-frances-ellen-watkins-harper-we-are-all-bound-together/.

58. Lepore, 319–330. The Chinese Exclusion Act would not be repealed until December 17, 1943.

59. *Frederick Douglass Papers*, 4:13.

60. Ernestine L. Rose, *A Defence of Atheism: a Lecture Delivered in Mercantile Hall, Boston*, April 10, 1861 (Boston: J. P. Mendum, 1881), 21.

61. Frederick Douglass, *Life and Times of Frederick Douglass* (New York: Library of America, 1994 [1882]), 906.

Chapter 4

Sowing Seeds and Harvesting Fruit

Women's Rights

More than a decade before Elizabeth Cady Stanton and Lucretia Mott helped to launch a women's right movement in Seneca Falls, New York in 1848, Ernestine Rose had been speaking out for women's rights. "I sent the first petition to the New York Legislature to give a married woman the right to hold real estate in her own name, in the winter of 1836–37,"[1] she recalled. Within a few years other activists joined her, collecting thousands of signatures that led to the passage of a groundbreaking women's property law in 1848 and to a more comprehensive "Married Woman's Property Act" in 1860.[2] Rose later remarked with some amusement: "Since the New York Legislature passed the above law, the papers speak of it as a very just movement and it would not much surprise me if they claim the merit of it as their own achievement!" How did Rose accomplish this transformation of public opinion? Her reply: "By agitation."[3]

Rose challenged women to turn their thoughts away from religion to the here and now, in order to consider their limited role in society and to take action to remedy this inequity. Rose gave one of her earliest recorded speeches on women's rights at the New England Social Reform Society Convention, an Owenite convention held in Boston in 1844. After speaking about Owenite socialist principles earlier at this convention, she turned to address the women in her audience:

> The clergy and the church don't recognize your right, my sisters, to speak publicly or in the church. Speak, then, not in their favor . . . What rights have women? . . . What of freedom have they? In government they are not known, but to be punished for breaking laws in which they have no voice in making. All avenues to enterprise and honor are closed against them. If poor, they must

drudge for a mere pittance—If of the wealthy classes, they must be dressed dolls of fashion—parlor puppets—female things. When single, they must be dependent on their parents or brothers, and when married, swallowed up in their husbands. Nothing of nobleness, dignity and elevation is allowed to exist in the female . . . A few are allowed to thrum the keys in a piano—to smatter a little French or Italian—to do cunning needlework . . . but then how masculine, indelicate and unwomanlike for her to pry into the heavier sciences—into the falsely—so-called sciences of politics and religion . . . This state of society does not recognize woman's equality . . . My sisters, speak out for yourselves.[4]

This excerpt from one of Rose's early women's rights speeches gives us insight into her rhetorical style and helps to explain what made her addresses so compelling. She used repetition of a rhetorical phrase, allowing its rhythmic power to drive home her message: "If poor, they must drudge . . . if of the wealthy classes, they must be dressed . . . "; "When single . . . when married . . . "; "—to thrum the keys in a piano—to smatter a little French . . . " Then, by progressing from the more impersonal, third-person form of address—"they"—to the second-person form, "you"—"My sisters, speak out for yourselves"—she communicated forcefully and directly with her listeners.

She criticized society's views on religion, for without "mental freedom," as she called it, there could be no social progress. Rose shocked her listeners with her anticlerical views in this speech, as when she admonished them: "I call upon you . . . never to enter a church again . . . They oppress you. They prevent progression. They are opposed to reason."

The audience's response to Rose's speech was immediate and extraordinary, according to one published report: "This appeal burst upon a listening throng like a thunderbolt, and they were instantly lashed into the wildest excitement of fury and applause. The door and passageway were crammed with spectators, most of them devotees of the church, and the speaker was assailed with a shower of hisses as fierce as though Pandemonium had let loose its metamorphosed angels upon a single woman!"

These interruptions continued throughout her speech. Advocating for women's rights was highly controversial in this era but criticizing the church was worse—it was considered taboo. This was an incendiary topic that provoked fury. Rose was one of the very rare reformers who chose to advocate for both intellectual freedom and women's rights, often addressing the two themes in her speeches.

When confronted with explosions of anger, catcalls and hisses during her speech, Rose refused to compromise or to appease her listeners. According to a published report, "Mrs. Rose waited calmly until the tumult had subsided, when she again repeated the injunction, and again the tumult rose still higher;

and the repetition and uproar went on until the excited multitude . . . was compelled, through exhaustion, to hear the daring heresy in silence."[5]

As a Jewish immigrant, freethinker and foreigner, Rose was both an outsider and insider among social reformers. At conventions, many orators would cite passages of scripture to support their views, and would incorporate Christian prayers into their addresses. Lucy Stone, Susan B. Anthony and Elizabeth Cady Stanton, all American-born Protestants, worked closely together; they were the leading triumvirate of women's rights activists. Lucretia Mott, a Quaker, alluded to Christianity's support for women's rights in her speeches and often concluded her lecture with a prayer.[6] Ernestine Rose, in contrast, would make references in her speeches to secular founding documents such as the Declaration of Independence.

She had more close friends from the freethought community than from her women's rights associates, although she did develop a lasting friendship with Susan B. Anthony. Stanton and Rose had similar views on female equality and abolition but their backgrounds differed greatly. Stanton's father was a wealthy judge in a family that had owned slaves. Stanton's privileged social status showed itself at times in her bias against foreigners and the less educated.[7]

When Antoinette Brown, the first ordained female minister in the United States, introduced a motion at a women's rights convention saying that the Bible endorsed female equality, Rose opposed her resolution. Rose argued that on the subject of human rights, "I see no need to appeal to any written authority, particularly when it is so obscure and indefinite as to admit of different interpretations." The convention supported her position. Despite their differences, Rose and Brown enjoyed a cordial relationship.[8]

Rose's European appearance and foreign accent caused some journalists to make racist and xenophobic comments, as when the editor of the *Albany Register* viciously attacked her after she had addressed the New York State Legislature on the subject of women's rights: "It is a melancholy reflection," opined the editor, "that among our American women who have been educated to better things, there should be found any who are willing to follow the lead of such foreign propagandists as the ringleted, glove-handed exotic, Ernestine L. Rose."[9] Surprisingly, even among women's rights activists there was prejudice against her. Lucy Stone said that she looked "too Jewish."[10] Rose stood out as well because of the many causes she supported: abolition of slavery, antiracism, freethought, religious freedom, women's rights and international human rights. By supporting a multitude of movements, she antagonized some Americans, including religious conservatives, Southern rights advocates and nativists.

Rose did not attend the 1848 Seneca Falls Convention, the earliest women's rights gathering, organized by Elizabeth Cady Stanton and Lucretia Mott. It had been organized on short notice and publicized only in local upstate New York newspapers.[11] She later paid tribute to the Declaration of Sentiments it produced: "It is no less great, noble and important, than the first honorable Declaration of Independence . . . and even more far-sighted and sublime. For . . . it was never before dreamed that woman would be included in it."[12]

One of the most prominent participants at the Seneca Falls Convention and at many later women's rights conventions was Frederick Douglass, who was a strong advocate of women's rights as well as an internationally known abolitionist. "As for myself, I dare not claim a right which I would not concede to women," Douglass proclaimed. "I would see her elevated to an equal position with man in every relation of life."[13] British and American antislavery women had raised funds to emancipate Douglass after he had escaped from slavery, helping him to establish a printing press and to become founding editor of an antislavery newspaper, *The North Star*. The motto of the *North Star* reflected his views on women's rights and on racial equality: "Right is of no Sex— Truth is of no Color—God is the Father of us all, and we are all Brethren."

Ernestine Rose gave one of the principal speeches at the First National Woman's Rights Convention, held in Worcester on October 23 and 24, 1850. More than 1,000 people came, mostly from the Northeast, but several from as far away as California, to attend this groundbreaking convention.[14] Conspicuously absent was Margaret Fuller, a prominent women's rights advocate, who had died tragically in a shipwreck on her return to America in July 1850, as she traveled home from Italy.

Attendees at the convention packed into Brinley Hall in Worcester, a city chosen because it was an important railroad hub and the second largest city in Massachusetts. According to an article in the *National Anti-Slavery Standard*, "The Hall was filled long before the hour" of the Convention and "every spot in the large room was filled with people standing in solid phalanx, where there were no seats.[15] Speakers included many reformers from the abolitionist movement such as William Lloyd Garrison, Paulina Wright Davis, Reverend William H. Channing, Lucretia Mott, Wendell Phillips, Lucy Stone, Ernestine Rose, Frederick Douglass and Sojourner Truth. The speakers and attendees represented a diverse cross-section of America—white middle-class Protestants, Black men and women of all social classes, including two former slaves, a foreign-born Jew, clergymen and lay people, believers, agnostics, atheists and freethinkers.

They had come together in Worcester to produce one of the most radical, egalitarian, antiracist agendas for human rights. Their resolutions would proclaim that all women and men of any color, whether enslaved or free, "had the same rights as any white man at the pinnacle of American society."[16] This demand for equality was based on the principles laid out in the Declaration of Independence and the Constitution. Rose called upon lawmakers to defend themselves for violating the fundamental principles of the republic or disprove their validity.

Instead of adopting a segregated approach to achieving women's legal and political rights, the Worcester Convention took a bold stand by creating an interracial coalition. Activists' views at this convention were all the more remarkable since this year saw the passage of the Fugitive Slave Act, which denied the humanity of Blacks by not allowing fugitives the right to a jury trial, and by requiring citizens to capture runaway slaves.

Paulina Wright Davis, President at the Worcester Convention, urged her listeners to focus on achieving results: "It is one thing to issue a declaration of rights or a declaration of wrongs to the world, but quite another thing . . . to secure the desired reformation."[17]

As Chair of the Business Committee, Rose was the author of at least one of the convention's resolutions, which she introduced: "We will not cease our earnest endeavors to secure for [women] political, legal and social equality with man, until her proper sphere is determined, by what alone should determine it—her Powers and Capacities, strengthened and refined by an education in accordance with her nature."[18] Throughout much of the nineteenth century, there was a widespread assumption that men and women were very distinctive from one another in physical and intellectual capacities and that each belonged in a separate sphere. Woman's sphere was a domestic one— marriage and childrearing—while a man's sphere was that of work, including politics, science and law. Rose and other feminists challenged this idea. They believed instead that men and women had similar natures and that social conditions, education, and cultural assumptions had resulted in women not living up to their full potential.

Rose spoke at the 1850 convention about the need for laws to be made equally for men and women, and for women to be educated "for the higher purposes of life. Why should she not be made acquainted with the arts, the sciences, and the philosophies of life? . . . Woman could study successfully any of the professions. This would be not so much for her benefit as for the benefit of the world."[19] As an Owenite, Rose held the view that social conditions formed human character, that women and men suffered from the current system and that both would benefit from a more egalitarian society. Her own successful, egalitarian marriage reinforced these views.

Frederick Douglass spoke about his own experiences as a Black man, "who had been turned out of railroad cars in Massachusetts, out of steamboat cabins, and knocked on the head." He said he had learned to "take his rights wherever he could get them—to assume them, at any rate, as properly his. . . . Women should take their rights. Seize hold of those which are most strongly contested . . . Let them strike out in some . . . path where they are not now allowed to go. Let Woman take her rights and then she shall be free."[20]

Douglass was arguing forcefully for women's assumption of their rights in the same way that he argued for Blacks' rights. He was a powerful role model for this act of seizing one's rights, based on his own life story. Having escaped from slavery, he educated himself and forged a career as a journalist and orator despite widespread prejudice against Blacks and despite almost insurmountable obstacles.

Another speaker who made a strong impression at the Worcester convention was Sojourner Truth, an itinerant evangelical preacher and abolitionist, born into slavery in New York, who had escaped in 1826. As the first Black woman to address a women's rights convention, she told the assembly, "If the treatment of women in this country was a proof of its civilization, the heathen would have to come yet and teach them civilization."[21] She would go on to address many other abolitionist and women's rights conventions, including one in Akron, Ohio in 1851, where she delivered her famous "Ain't I a Woman?" speech, in which she spoke of discrimination against Black women.[22]

The 1850 Convention produced the following important resolutions:

Resolved, that every human being of full age, and resident for a proper length of time on the soil of the nation, who is required to obey law, is entitled to a voice in its enactments.

Resolved, that women are entitled to the right of suffrage and to be considered eligible for office; that every party which claims to represent humanity, civilization and progress of the age [should proclaim] equality before the law, without distinction of sex or color.

Resolved, that political rights acknowledge no sex, and therefore the word 'male' should be stricken from every State Constitution.

Resolved, that the laws of property as affecting married parties . . . [should] be equal between them.[23]

The reformers who gathered in Worcester in 1850 had a vision far ahead of mainstream thinking. They were challenging America to uphold its egalitarian principles or to cease proclaiming itself a liberal democracy. The abolitionist press praised the convention, saying that "Mrs. Ernestine Rose spoke with great eloquence . . . Her French [sic] accent and extemporaneous manner added quite a charm to her animated and forcible style."[24]

Other newspaper accounts heaped scorn on the event. The *New York Herald*'s editorial of October 26, 1850 gave an overtly racist account of Sojourner Truth's speech, conveying a sense of threat that the journalist felt regarding the notion of racial and gender equality:

Mrs. Sojourner Truth . . . next came forward. And why not? In a convention where sex and color are mingled together in the common rights of humanity,

Dinah, and Burleigh, and Lucretia, and Frederick Douglas[s], are all spiritually of one color and one sex, and all on a perfect footing of reciprocity. Most assuredly, Dinah was well posted up on the rights of woman, and . . . she contended for her right to vote, to hold office, to practice medicine and the law, and to wear the breeches with the best white man that walks upon God's earth.[25]

The above writer referred to Sojourner Truth by the generic racist term, "Dinah," scorning her for advocating for equality. His words reflected the widespread prejudice against Blacks in much of the nation.

Another journalist from the *New York Herald* expressed outrage: "Now let us see what all this balderdash, clap-trap, moonshine, rant, cant, fanaticism and blasphemy, means."[26] Despite the mockery, anger and scorn in many newspaper accounts, the convention proved that "no press is bad press." The 1850 National Woman's Rights Convention drew attention to the issues of women's rights and racial equality, helped to win some converts and launched a national movement, the first in the world.[27]

The following year, three thousand people attended the Second National Woman's Rights Convention, held in Worcester City Hall to accommodate the larger crowd. Reflecting the growing consensus that suffrage was essential, Wendell Phillips, a well-known abolitionist and women's rights supporter, entitled his address, "Shall Women Have the Right to Vote?" and introduced the following as his first resolution, which would win the convention's support: "Resolved, that, while we would not undervalue other methods, the right of suffrage for women is, in our opinion, the cornerstone of this enterprise, since we do not seek to protect woman, but rather to place her in a position to protect herself."[28]

By the Second National Convention, Ernestine Rose had become recognized as central to the movement. She gave the convention's principal address, focusing on the obstacles, misconceptions and prejudices about women that had prevented them from occupying their rightful place in society. Rose masterfully used facts, logic, anecdotes and satire as rhetorical strategies to persuade her listeners to join her in taking "the grandest step in the onward progress of humanity." She appealed to rationalist arguments for women's rights, turning to America's founding documents:

Here, in this far-famed land of freedom, under a Republic that has inscribed on its banner the great truth that all men are created free and equal, and endowed with inalienable rights to life, liberty and the pursuit of happiness . . . woman, the mockingly so-called 'better half' of man, has yet to plead for her rights, nay, for her life, for what is life without liberty? . . . Is she then not included in that declaration? . . . Why, in the name of reason and justice, why should she not have the same rights?

Then came her compelling articulation of her main thesis:

Humanity recognizes no sex—virtue recognizes no sex—mind recognizes no sex—life and death, pleasure and pain, happiness and misery recognize no sex. Like man, woman comes involuntarily into existence, like him she possesses physical and mental and moral powers, on the proper cultivation of which depends her happiness; like him she is subject to all the vicissitudes of life; like him she has to pay the penalty for disobeying nature's laws . . . like him she enjoys or suffers with her country.

Rose was appealing to both head and heart. Having laid out arguments for women's rights based on natural rights guaranteed by the Declaration of Independence, Rose gave her most powerful arguments in succinct phrases, using repetition as a rhetorical device: . . . . "recognizes no sex . . . "recognizes no sex" . . . "like him . . . like him," to drive home her message that women and men's common humanity far outweighed any differences between the two sexes. They both had the same potential for self-development if they were given the right social conditions. Ignorance and false cultural assumptions on the part of both men and women kept women from assuming a larger role in society. Rose then articulated the future benefits for society: "If she can take her stand by his side . . . in the Legislative halls, in the Senate chamber, in the Judge's chair, in the jury box, in the Forum, in the Laboratory of the arts and sciences, and wherever duty would call her for the benefit of herself, her country, her race. . . . At every step she would carry with her a humanizing influence." She argued for women's rights not for women alone, but rather as a benefit for all of humanity.

Rose shifted to a lighter tone when she spoke about men's preferences for delicate, sickly women: "Not physical and mental vigor, but a pale, delicate face, hands too small to grasp a broom, for that were treason in a lady; a voice so sentimental and depressed, that what she says can be learned only by the moving of her half-parted lips, and above all, that nervous sensibility which sees a ghost in every passing shadow . . . that shrinking mock modesty that faints at the mention of a leg of a table."[29]

She would speak thereafter at nearly every national and state women's rights convention until she moved to Europe in 1869. The speech that Rose delivered at the 1851 National Convention would never be forgotten. Paulina Wright Davis later described it this way: "Mrs. Ernestine L. Rose made an address of an hour in length, which has never been surpassed."[30]

The 1850's was a decade of intense activism in both women's rights and antislavery movements, with conventions timed so that reform-minded people could attend both. Attendees ranged from activists, reformers, curiosity seekers and those opposed to rights for women and Blacks, who came for the express purpose of disrupting meetings and mocking speakers. Publicity and newspaper accounts, both negative and positive, helped to generate growing interest in these movements, which over time would slowly move popular opinion in favor of more progressive laws.

Rose spoke of the principle of justice as a basis for all human rights at the Third National Woman's Rights Convention in 1852 when she argued, "We ask not for our rights as a gift of charity, but as an act of justice . . . That as she is amenable to the laws of her country, she is entitled to a voice in their enactment, and to all the protective advantages they can bestow . . . Any difference, therefore, in political, civil and social rights, on account of sex, is in direct violation of the principles of justice and humanity . . . "[31] She was drawing here on her Jewish upbringing, which had taught her the ethical principle of *tzedakah*—"righteousness."

She argued with Reverend Antoinette L. Brown over the issue of biblical justification for women's rights. Rose's references to American history made her arguments more persuasive:

> When the inhabitants of Boston converted their harbor into a tea-pot, rather than submit to unjust taxes, they did not go to the Bible for their authority; for if they had, they would have been told from the same authority to "give unto Caesar what belonged to Caesar." Had the people, when they rose in the might of their right to throw off the British yoke, appealed to the Bible for authority, it would have answered them, "submit to the powers that be, for they are from God." No! On Human rights and Freedom . . . there is no need of any written authority.[32]

New York City became the site of the first World's Fair to be held in the United States in 1853. Crowds were drawn to a newly constructed Crystal Palace which resembled London's famous structure. Many of them were also drawn to the women's rights convention held at the Broadway Tabernacle in Manhattan on September 8 and 9. Rowdy attendees created such bedlam and disruption that it was nicknamed the "Mob Convention." Rose focused her remarks on the married women's property laws in New York State and spoke of her petitions presented to the Legislature. Frederick Douglass initially disagreed with Rose's arguments: "Who is to decide in a disagreement touching the property rights of the husband and wife? Man was best qualified to be the person to decide." Rose continued to argue for giving husband and wife equal rights in decision making. Douglass, ultimately persuaded by Rose and other women's rights activists, would later actively fight for women's property rights in the New York State Legislature.[33]

Rose continued to attract large crowds and to receive mostly favorable newspaper reviews of her speeches. She was elected president at the Fifth National Woman's Rights Convention in 1854, held in Philadelphia. Rose argued that both men's and women's rights were conceded by that "first great and immutable truth . . . that all men are created equal . . . " Her strategy was to challenge her opponents to respond in an open debate:

> On these grounds we ask man to meet us, and meet us in the spirit of inquiry . . . and if they can, to convince us that we are not included in that great Declaration of Independence; that although it is a right principle that taxation and representation are inseparable, yet woman ought to be taxed, and ought not to be represented; and that although it is an acknowledged principle that all just power of government is derived from the consent of the governed, yet woman should be governed without her consent. Let them meet us fairly and openly. . . . and we will hear them. If they can convince us that we are wrong, we will give up our claims; but if we can convince them that we are right in claiming our rights, as they are in claiming theirs, then we expect them in a spirit of candor and honesty to acknowledge it.[34]

Rose believed that through rational discourse and spirited debate, social change would ultimately come about, since it was the false cultural assumptions about men and women and institutions supporting them that hampered progress. The *Albany Express* wrote of her address at this convention, "This woman . . . is a remarkable one. She possesses an intellect that lifts her 'head and shoulders' above the mass of her sex."[35] The *New York Tribune* praised her eloquence, saying that her addresses "showed wide experience and a more highly cultivated mind, perhaps, than any of the other ladies present."[36]

The *Albany Register*, on the other hand, attacked Rose with vicious invective after she had addressed the New York State Legislature that same year, revealing the paper's anti-immigrant, sexist and anti-Semitic biases:

> In no other country in the world . . . would her infidel propagandism and preachings . . . be tolerated. She would be prohibited . . . from her efforts to obliterate from the world the religion of the Cross . . . It never was contemplated that these exotic agitators would come up to our legislators and ask for the passage of laws upholding and sanctioning their wild and foolish doctrines.

In response to this verbal attack, Rose defended herself and other reformers in a letter to the editor of the *Albany Register*. She addressed the editor's xenophobia by reminding him that her countrymen had played an important role in assisting Americans during their struggle for independence. She was referring to the Polish émigré General Thaddeus Kosciuszko, who had come to the aid of the Continental Army:

> Everyone who ever advanced a new idea, no matter how great and noble, has been subjected to criticism, and therefore we too must expect it . . . No true soul

will ever be deterred from the performance of a duty by any criticism . . . I chose to make this country my home, in preference to any other, because if you carried out the theories you profess, it would indeed be the noblest country on earth. And as my countrymen so nobly aided in the physical struggle for Freedom and Independence, I felt, and still feel it equally my duty to use my humble abilities to the uttermost in my power, to aid in the great moral struggle for human rights and human freedom.[37]

In recognition of Ernestine Rose's growing fame as an orator, a Cleveland journalist, Lemuel E. Barnard, interviewed her and published her biographical sketch in the *Excelsior* in 1856.[38]

Rose's health began to decline in the late 1850's and she was unable to maintain the full travel schedule she had previously held. She would write about dizziness that came and went, and later wrote that she suffered from neuralgia in her "head, chest and the whole upper part of [her] body."[39] The *Boston Investigator* told its readers in 1859, "She [Rose] has for some time been failing in health." A journalist, Sara Underwood, wrote that since returning to America from a trip to Europe in 1856, "her health was so poor and uncertain that she was obliged to forbear taking much active part in the reforms so dear to her."[40]

She seemed to recover some of her strength and spirit at the Tenth National Woman's Rights Convention in 1860, when she spoke of growing support for women's rights and of expanded women's employment opportunities:

Already the Woman's Rights platform has upon it lawyers, ministers, and statesmen—men who are among the highest in the nation. I need not mention a William Lloyd Garrison or a Wendell Phillips; but there are others . . . who have stood upon our platform. Who would have expected it? . . . Beecher [Reverend Henry Ward Beecher]! Think of it for a moment! A minister advocating the rights of woman, even her right at the ballot-box! . . . Then there has been a great enlargement of the industrial sphere of woman . . . Many are now engaged in printing offices as type-setters . . . Dry good stores, fancy stores . . . The soil is waiting for [man's] plough. And so it is waiting for women. Not only the physical, but the social soil is awaiting the plough, wielded by woman's heart and head.[41]

With the election of President Abraham Lincoln in November 1860, followed by the secession of Southern states to form the Confederate States of America, discussions and conventions related to women's rights were suspended. Four long, bloody years of the Civil War ensued. Lincoln took the momentous step on January 1, 1863 of issuing the Emancipation Proclamation, which ended slavery in the Confederate states.

Susan B. Anthony, Elizabeth Cady Stanton, Lucy Stone and Ernestine L. Rose organized the Women's Loyal National League to contribute to the war effort and to support a constitutional amendment that would guarantee slavery's extinction. They drew up a petition that collected 400,000 signatures for Congress. Senator Charles Sumner credited the work of this group of women with the passage of the Thirteenth Amendment, abolishing slavery throughout the United States. President Lincoln signed the resolution but tragically did not live to see the ratification of the Thirteenth Amendment. John Wilkes Booth assassinated him on Good Friday, April 14, 1865.

The nation was shaken and grief stricken. Stores throughout cities and towns were shuttered and draped in black crepe. "There was not a store on Broadway that was not draped in deep black, mingled with pure white," wrote the *New York World*.[42] Lincoln's funeral train left Washington on April 21 and made its way to Baltimore, Harrisburg, Philadelphia, and to Manhattan, where his body was placed in a hearse drawn by six gray horses. The procession made its way down Broadway to a black-draped City Hall. Lines of people formed to pay their last respects.[43]

After the Union victory in 1865, it appeared for a few years that both women and Blacks would be given political rights, including the franchise. These hopes would soon be dashed. The Republican Party would turn its energy away from race relations and reform, toward economic growth and industrialization.[44] The historical moment of innovative legislation was passing, followed by a period that emphasized order, stability and protection of the status quo.[45]

As Congress was considering the Fourteenth Amendment in 1865, suffragists began to grow anxious. While Section 1 conferred citizenship on all persons—both male and female—born or naturalized in the United States, Section 2 would penalize states if they withheld the vote from any male citizen who was at least twenty-one years old. This clause introduced gender distinction for the first time into the American Constitution.

The Reconstruction era following the Civil War would prove to be divisive and difficult for the women's movement, as they split over whether Black men should be given the vote before women. At the Eleventh National Woman's Rights Convention in 1866, participants created a new association—the American Equal Rights Association—which was dedicated to securing "equal rights to all American citizens, especially the right of suffrage, irrespective of race, color or sex." It was an effort to merge the cause of women's rights with that of Blacks. Lucretia Mott was elected president. Frances Ellen Watkins Harper, a poet and abolitionist, spoke of the plight of Black women and called for universal suffrage: "You white women speak here of rights," she stated. "I speak of wrongs. I, as a colored woman, have had in this country an education which has made me feel as if I were in the situation of Ishmael."[46]

Two factions would emerge from the old abolitionist-feminist coalition, divided over the proposed Fifteenth Amendment, which stated that the right to vote could not be denied on the basis of "race, color, or previous condition of servitude," thereby excluding women from enfranchisement. One group, supported by Rose, Anthony, Stanton, Mott and Davis, wanted universal suffrage. The second group, supported by Phillips, Douglass, Garrison, Foster and Kelley, prioritized Black male suffrage over female suffrage in the short term, while advocating for women's suffrage at a later time.

The Republican Party called it "the Negro's hour." Frederick Douglass and others in this group said that linking women's suffrage with Black suffrage would lessen the chances of securing the ballot for Black men. Douglass said that while he wanted the ballot for both men and women, "I don't see how anyone can pretend that there is the same urgency in giving the ballot to woman as to the Negro. With us, the matter is a question of life and death."[47] When President Andrew Johnson implemented his own version of Reconstruction policies, he did not prevent Southern states from passing Black Codes, depriving Blacks of their civil liberties. Hate crimes, including lynching of Blacks by the Ku Klux Klan, were becoming more widespread. Federal intervention in the early 1870's would suppress the Ku Klux Klan without completely eliminating it.[48]

Ernestine Rose gave an impassioned speech at the First Anniversary of the American Equal Rights Association in 1867 in which she quoted from Lincoln. She used the metaphor of a house—"a house divided against itself cannot stand"—to argue that America as a republic had been built from the beginning on a faulty foundation:

> It discriminated against color; it discriminated against woman; and at the same time it pronounced that all men were created free and equal . . . It raised its superstructure to the clouds; and it has fallen as low as any empire could fall. It is divided. A house divided against itself cannot stand. A wrong always operates against itself, and falls back on the wrong-doer. We have proclaimed to the world universal suffrage; but it is universal suffrage . . . excluding the Negro and the woman, who are by far the largest majority in this country.

The Reconstruction era was an opportunity, in Rose's opinion, to rebuild the nation on a sound foundation that included equal rights for all.

Rose showed in her address at the 1867 convention a modern understanding of the connection between political power and money. She said, amid laughter and applause, "Give us one million of [sic] dollars, and we will have the elective franchise at the very next session of our Legislature." Since women didn't have political clout or dollars, all they could do was to raise their voices in order to influence public opinion and legislators.[49]

The debate over the proposed Fifteenth Amendment deepened the division between two former allies, feminists and abolitionists, stirring hostility between the two groups at an American Equal Rights Association meeting in May 1869. Using language that was increasingly bitter and racist, some suffragists made the campaign into a class and race struggle, which pitted educated white women against uneducated Black men and immigrants. Elizabeth Cady Stanton, opposed to the Fifteenth Amendment, angered Frederick Douglass and other abolitionists when she published editorials in the women's rights newspaper, *The Revolution*, saying that before the "ignorant Black man" should be given the ballot, intelligent and cultured white women should be enfranchised.[50] George Francis Train, an openly racist, wealthy Democrat, had given Stanton and Anthony critically needed financial support for *The Revolution*. The newspaper's inflammatory rhetoric alienated Black women and men and impeded progress towards gaining the ballot for women.[51] Stanton spoke in racist terms about foreigners and Blacks who would be allowed to vote before women received the ballot:

> What may [women] be called to endure when all the lower orders of foreigners now crowding our shores legislate for them and their daughters? Think of Patrick and Sambo and Hans and Yung Tung, who do not know the difference between a monarchy and a republic, who cannot read the Declaration of Independence or Webster's spelling-book, making laws for Lucretia Mott, Ernestine L. Rose, and Anna E. Dickinson.[52]

Rose never spoke about denying Black men the ballot and she struggled to maintain a discourse focused on universal rights amid growing hostility between the two factions. "Why is it my friends that Congress has enacted laws to give the Negro of the South the right to vote?" she asked. "Why do they not at the same time protect the Negro woman?"[53] Rose had always believed that giving full rights to all races and to both men and women was the only right course to follow. She argued: "It has been justly stated that the Negro at present suffers more than woman, but it can do him no injury to place woman in the same category with him . . . It can do no injury, but must do good . . . "[54]

She continued to press for universal suffrage: "There could be no safety to the rights of women until they possessed the ballot. I do not war with man, but with bad principles." Rose appealed for the ballot, "the little talisman," to be placed in the hands of woman. She mocked legislators: "We asked what [Congress] meant by 'impartial suffrage.' They said, 'Why man, of course, man and his brother.' They don't speak of woman and her sisters. We might commence by calling the Chinaman a man and a brother, or the Hottentot or the Calmuck or the Indian, the idiot or the criminal, but where shall we stop? They will bring all these in before us, and then they will bring in the babies— the male babies (Laughter)."[55] Amid growing tensions and frustration over the refusal of Congress to pass an amendment for universal suffrage, Rose had said the only racist comment of hers ever recorded, spoken as a joke—words that went against her strong commitment to universal human rights. She could not accept the argument of postponing equal rights for men and women in order to ratify the Fifteenth Amendment, since that would compromise her principles.

During the May 14 meeting of the Equal Rights Association, Rose raised another important issue—that of unequal pay for women and men. Noting that working women received inadequate pay, she spoke of the importance of creating "cooperative societies" to advocate for women's labor rights.[56] At a meeting of the newly formed Workingwomen's Association, she had earlier advised them to become incorporated and to establish a savings bank and insurance company.[57] The subject of unequal wages and benefits for women and men would persist, and activists would continue, for decades, to press Congress for laws that would address this inequity, in the twentieth and twenty-first centuries.

After several stormy meetings in 1869, the women's rights movement split into two groups: the National Woman Suffrage Association, co-founded by Rose, Stanton and Anthony, and the American Woman Suffrage Association, founded by Lucy Stone. Rose must have realized then that there was no longer a chance to achieve universal suffrage during this turbulent period. However, states would continue their own battles for women's suffrage. According to one scholar, "Rose, more than any other individual, is credited with responsibility for Wyoming's adoption of women's suffrage in 1869— the first such law in all the American states and territories."[58]

Nationalism, xenophobia, anti-Semitism and religious conservatism marked the period following the Civil War years, as a new generation of reformers began to take center stage in America. Among these suffragists, some were opposed to giving equal voting rights to foreign-born Americans, Blacks and non-Protestants; others were opposed to giving the franchise to uneducated citizens. According to an historian, some suffragists had a "worldview replete with racial bigotry, religious and moral arrogance, class biases and a nearly complete disregard for non-Western peoples."[59] Carrie Chapman Catt, a suffragist, warned of the danger of "votes possessed by the male in the slums" . . . and of the "ignorant foreign vote." Belle Kearney, a Mississippi suffragist, decried the "enormity of the race question . . . when 4,500,000 ex-slaves, illiterate and semi-barbarous, were enfranchised."

According to Kearney, "Anglo-Saxonism . . . was the standard of the ages to
come and the granite foundation of the South."[60]

Many women's rights advocates dissociated themselves from Rose because
of her Jewish origins and strong antireligious views. She was more than ever
an outcast among members of this younger generation of racist and xenophobic reformers. Susan B. Anthony was admonished by one of the leading male
reform figures: "You would better never hold another convention than allow
Ernestine Rose on your platform." Anthony, loyal to her close friend, stood
firmly by Rose, later saying, "Did we banish Mrs. Rose? No, indeed!"[61]

The two groups would feud for twenty-one years until they reunited in
1890 as the National American Woman Suffrage Association. A new generation of men and women would continue their battle for universal suffrage
until 1920, when passage of the Nineteenth Amendment would at last grant
women the right to vote. The struggle for universal voting rights would by no
means be over, though. In 1965, President Lyndon B. Johnson would sign into
law the Voting Rights Act to help overcome legal barriers preventing many
Blacks from voting. The twenty-first century would see the passage of new
state laws that would make it more difficult for minorities to vote.

Ernestine and William Rose left the United States, moving to England in
1869, just a few weeks after the stormy split of the two women's suffrage
movements. She never explained their motive for leaving the country. In
addition to her growing health issues—rheumatism, neuralgia and lung problems—she must have been disturbed and exhausted by the growing strife
among reformers and by the openly racist and anti-immigrant rhetoric among
them. It was a far cry from her principle of human rights for all. Rose could
never accept the notion that the rights of one group of people took precedence
over that of another group and she would never compromise on this.

Activists in both women's suffrage movements would soon reconcile with
Frederick Douglass. He would often speak at their conventions during the
following decades and would pay tribute to the contributions of women to
the struggle for a more democratic nation. Mrs. Fannie Cooper, leader of the
women's rights movement in Philadelphia, would later say of Douglass in her
eulogy, following his death: "We have lost the most conspicuous advocate of
our rights, by the death of Frederick Douglass."[62]

When William and Ernestine Rose returned for ten months to visit the
United States in 1873–1874, Rose spoke at a meeting of the National Woman
Suffrage Association. She was full of hope for the future of the women's
rights movement: "The difference in public opinion and the condition of
women when [we] proclaimed women's rights thirty-eight years ago [is]
amazing. Remembering, also, that from the earliest ages of the human race,
false ideas regarding women have prevailed, the progress in these few years
is wonderful."[63] She would later write a letter to Susan B. Anthony, to be read

aloud at the thirtieth anniversary celebration of the women's rights movement in 1878:

> Go on, go on, halt not and rest not. Remember that 'eternal vigilance is the price
> of liberty' and of right. Much has been achieved; but the main, the vital thing,
> has yet to come. The suffrage is the magic key to the statute—the insignia of
> citizenship in a republic.[64]

With their move to England, the Roses would continue to advocate for
human rights. Ernestine Rose would resume her activism in Europe for
freethought, women's rights, international human rights, and for peace, as
outspoken and fearless as ever.

NOTES

1. Ernestine L. Rose, quoted in Elizabeth Cady Stanton, Susan B. Anthony, Matilda
Joslyn Gage, eds., *History of Woman Suffrage*, vol. 1: 100, Gutenberg E-book.

2. Paula Doress-Worters, ed., *Mistress of Herself: Speeches and Letters of Ernestine L. Rose, Early Women's Rights Leader* (New York: The Feminist Press, 2008), 11.

3. Ernestine L. Rose,"Letter to the Editor with Text of the New York State Married
Woman's Property Act," *Boston Investigator*, March 28, 1860, in Doress-Worters,
255–259.

4. Ernestine L. Rose, "Speech at the New England Social Reform Society Convention," May 30, 1844, Boston, quoted in Doress-Worters, 63–64.

5. Doress-Worters, 63–64.

6. See for example Lucretia Mott's concluding remarks: "And now, Lord, let thy
servants depart in peace; for our eyes have seen thy salvation," cited in "Women's
Rights Convention," *National Anti-Slavery Standard,* October 31, 1850.

7. See Stanton's remarks at the American Equal Rights Association meeting in May
1869, discussed later in this chapter and in footnote 52, explaining her opposition to
the Fifteenth Amendment.

8. Ernestine L. Rose, "Debate at the Third National Woman's Rights Convention,"
September 9, 1852, in Doress-Worters, 123–125.

9. "Woman's Rights in the Legislature," *Albany Register*, March 6, 1854, in
Doress-Worters,165–166.

10. Lucy Stone, "Letter to Susan B. Anthony," November 2, 1855, in *Stanton
and Anthony Papers*, microfilm, reel 8, frames 298–309; Blackwell Family Papers,
Library of Congress.

11. Bonnie S. Anderson, *The Rabbi's Atheist Daughter: Ernestine Rose, International Feminist Pioneer* (New York: Oxford University Press, 2017), 69.

12. Ernestine L. Rose,"Speech at the Fourth National Woman's Rights Convention," October 7, 1853, in Doress-Worters, 158.

13. Frederick Douglass,"Woman's Rights Convention," *The North Star*, August 11, 1848.

14. Ernestine L. Rose,"Resolution and Speech at the First National Woman's Rights Convention," October 23, 1850, in Doress-Worters, 80–81.

15. "Woman's Rights Convention at Worcester,"*National Anti-Slavery Standard*, October 31, 1850.

16. Lisa Connelly Cook, "The Radical Egalitarian Agenda of the First National Woman's Rights Convention of 1850" (MA Thesis, Clark University, 1998) in Worcester Women's History Project, https://www.wwhp.org.

17. "Woman's Rights Convention," *Standard*.

18. Ernestine L. Rose,Resolution and Speech at the First National Woman's Rights Convention," in Doress-Worters, 81–82.

19. "Woman's Rights Convention," *Standard*.

20. "Woman's Rights Convention," *Standard*.

21. Sojourner Truth, quoted in Barbara F. Berenson, *Massachusetts in the Woman Suffrage Movement* (Charleston: The History Press, 2018), 37.

22. Berenson, 37.

23. "Woman's Rights Convention," *Standard*.

24. "Woman's Rights Convention," *Standard*.

25. "Editorial,"*New York Herald*, October 26, 1850, cited by Cook, "The Radical Egalitarian Agenda."

26. James Gordon Bennett, "Editorial," *New York Herald*, October 28, 1850, cited by Cook.

27. According to historian Arvonne S. Fraser, "Organizing for political purposes was the major contribution of American women to the development of women's human rights [worldwide]." See Arvonne S. Fraser, "Becoming Human: The Origins and Development of Women's Human Rights," *Human Rights Quarterly* 21, no. 4 (November 1999): 872.

28. Wendell Phillips, "Shall women have the right to vote?" Address given in Worcester, MA, 1851, in Worcester Women's History Project, https://www.wwhp.org.

29. Ernestine L. Rose, "Speeches at the Second National Woman's Rights Convention," October 15–16, 1851, in Doress-Worters, 92–100.

30. Doress-Worters, 91.

31. Ernestine L. Rose, "Debate at the Third National Woman's Rights Convention," September 9, 1852, in Doress-Worters, 126.

32. Doress-Worters, 125–126.

33. Ernestine L. Rose, "Speeches at the New York State Woman's Rights Convention," in Doress-Worters, 153–156; Frederick Douglass, "Women's Rights Convention," *Frederick Douglass Paper,* December 16, 1853; Philip S. Foner, ed., *Frederick Douglass on Women's Rights* (Westport: Greenwood Press, 1976), 18.

34. Ernestine L. Rose, "Speech at the Fifth National Woman's Rights Convention," October 18, 1854, in Doress-Worters, 179–180.

35. "Mrs. Ernestine L. Rose," *The Liberator,* April 7, 1854.

36. Ernestine L. Rose, "Speech at the Fifth National Woman's Rights Convention," in Doress-Worters, 179.

37. "Attack in the *Albany Register* and Ernestine L. Rose's Response," March 6–7, 1854, in Doress-Worters, 165–168.

38. L. E. Barnard, "Ernestine L. Rose," the *Excelsior,* reprinted in *The Liberator,* May 16, 1856.

39. Anderson, 155.

40. *Boston Investigator*, March 23, 1859, 3; Sara A. Underwood, "Ernestine L. Rose," *Heroines of Free Thought* (New York: C. P. Somerby, 1876), 273.

41. Ernestine L. Rose, "Speech at the Tenth National Woman's Rights Convention," May 10, 1860, in Doress-Worters, 264–265.

42. *New York World*, April 20, 1865; Anderson, 131–132.

43. Edwin G. Burrows and Mike Wallace, *Gotham: A History of New York City to 1898* (New York: Oxford University Press, 1999), 904.

44. Berenson, 55.

45. David W. Blight, *Race and Reunion: The Civil War in American Memory* (Cambridge: Harvard University Press, 2001), 98–99.

46. Frances Ellen Watkins Harper, "We Are All Bound up Together," Address given at the Eleventh National Women's Rights Convention in New York City in 1866, quoted in Berenson, 47, https://www.blackpast.org/african-american-history/speeches-african-american-history/1866-frances-ellen-watkins-harper-we-are-all-bound-together/.

47. Stanton, Anthony, and Gage, eds., *History of Woman Suffrage*, vol. 2: 382, Project Gutenberg E-book.

48. Philip S. Foner, ed., *Frederick Douglass on Women's Rights* (Westport: Greenwood Press, 1976), 31–32; Blight, 112–114.

49. Ernestine L. Rose, "Speech at the First Anniversary of the American Equal Rights Association," May 10, 1867, in Doress-Worters, 335–336.

50. Stanton, Anthony, and Gage, eds., *History of Woman Suffrage*, vol. 2: 353.

51. Berenson, 48–49.

52. Stanton, Anthony and Gage, vol. 2: 353.

53. Stanton, Anthony and Gage, vol. 2: 396.

54. Ernestine L. Rose, "Speeches at the National Convention of the Loyal Women of the Republic," May 14, 1863, in Doress-Worters, 304.

55. Stanton, Anthony and Gage, Vol. 2, 396–397.

56. "Equal Rights: Another Interesting Debate by Female Suffrage Agitators," *New York Times*, May 14, 1869, 8.

57. "Workingwomen's Association," *New York Times*, January 9, 1869, 8.

58. Stanley R. Brav, "The Jewish Woman, 1861–1865," *American Jewish Archives Journal* 17, no. 1 (1965): footnote,74.

59. Lori D. Ginzberg, "Re-viewing the First Wave," *Feminist Studies* 28, no. 2 (Summer 2002), Gale General OneFile.

60. Aileen S. Kraditor, *Up From the Pedestal: Selected Writings in the History of American Feminism* (Chicago: Quadrangle, 1968), 257–258, 261–265.

61. Ida H. Harper, *The Life and Work of Susan B. Anthony,* vol. 1:853 (Indianapolis: Bowen-Merrill, 1899).

62. Foner, 40, 43.

63. "Mr. and Mrs. Rose," *Boston Investigator*, May 27, 1874.

64. Ernestine L. Rose, "Letter to the National Woman Suffrage Association Convention," July 19, 1878, in Doress-Worters, 350.

Ernestine Rose (1810–1892),
holding a book, taken in 1856.
*Schlesinger Library, Radcliffe
Institute, Harvard University.*

Engraving of Ernestine Rose from a daguerreotype. *Collection of the Massachusetts
Historical Society, 81.565. Used with
permission.*

Lithograph of Ernestine Rose by Leopold Grozelier, 1856. Rose is holding a scroll, perhaps representing a petition or law. *Library of Congress LC-USZ62-52045.*

Frederick Douglass (1818–1895), c. 1847–1852,
by Samuel J. Miller. *Original image at the Art
Institute of Chicago.*

Sojourner Truth (1799–1883), 1864. *Courtesy of the* Library *of* Congress. *https://www.loc.gov/item/rbcmiller001306/.*

"The Champions of Woman's Suffrage," *Harper's Bazar,* June 12, 1869, 38.
Division of Rare and Manuscript Collections, Cornell University Library.

Elizabeth Cady Stanton (1815–1902) and Susan B.
Anthony (1820–1906), c. 1870. *National Portrait Gallery,
Smithsonian Institution, Washington, DC. S/NPG.77.48.*

Chapter 5

The World Is My Country

Ernestine Rose introduced herself to the American public as a "foreigner" at a time when this nation was torn apart by deepening sectional strife and by nativist sentiments. She saw her adopted country differently from many native-born Americans, since growing up in Poland she had experienced foreign occupation, oppression and persecution. There were few Polish immigrants living in the United States in the mid-nineteenth century, so Rose was most likely not part of a cohesive ethnic group. She acted as an individual before joining any organized movements in her many battles for human rights.[1]

She would often speak of her vision of America as a nation that would play a prominent role in world affairs, support democracy, help to defeat authoritarian regimes, offer asylum to political refugees and immigrants, and serve as a bastion of freedom and equality. Rose would continually remind her listeners of the democratic ideals that America stood for and of its important role as a model for other nations struggling against tyranny.

Rose saw the interconnectedness of the different causes she supported—abolition, antiracism , women's rights, freethought, religious freedom—all of them part of a global struggle for human rights, whose goal was to give full social, economic and political rights to everyone so that each person could "perfect himself [and herself] in that most important of all educations, the knowledge of himself and of society."[2] She was a visionary leader who sought to raise public awareness of international issues, and who linked human rights movements at home to those in Europe. The two years she had spent in Germany as a young adult had introduced her to the Enlightenment; her stay in France and in England had given her insight into social inequities. This broad European perspective would stay with her throughout her adult life.

At a Thomas Paine Celebration in 1849, Rose spoke of the many revolutions that were sweeping across Europe—in France, Poland, Hungary, Germany and Italy—as these countries attempted to overthrow monarchies and install democratic regimes: "Liberty, Equality, Fraternity, that glorious trinity . . . has caused thrones to shake, scepters to bow down, and miters to be crushed. Kings and priests tremble before this newborn messenger of peace." Rose told her audience that although she was not an advocate of war or violence, she identified with the suffering nations of Europe: "Look at poor, downtrodden Ireland! . . . [My] heart sickens in contemplating the scenes of horror that have been perpetrated on poor humanity. And why all this? Because man claimed his birthright, liberty."

Connecting the struggles for freedom abroad with the women's rights movement at home, she argued: "Liberty cannot exist without equality of rights . . . Whenever liberty shall be based on equality, the only sound basis upon which a true republic can rest, then man will . . . recognize in every man a brother, and in every woman a sister . . . Man can never be truly free until woman has her rights as his equal . . . "[3]

Rose's speeches showed her knowledge of contemporary political events in Europe and her understanding of the relevance of European affairs to America. She reminded Americans in her 1850 Paine speech that our country, having benefited from foreigners who had intervened during the American Revolution, should therefore repay the debt it owed to Europe by supporting European leaders struggling to liberate their nations from despotism:

> It would be well to remember that Paine, Lafayette, Kosciuszko and many other noble minds who enlisted in the cause of right over might, were foreigners; and that this country owes a debt of gratitude which now is the time to pay. Every sympathy, encouragement and means of help ought to be extended towards those brave and faithful men . . . those, who, for the cause of Freedom—the cause of Truth—have to sacrifice home, wealth, friends, all that makes life desirable, and become strangers and wanderers in foreign lands.

She pressed her listeners to support petitions to Congress in order to give asylum to revolutionary leaders such as Louis Kossuth of Hungary, Józef Bem of Poland and Guiseppe Mazzini of Italy, fleeing tyranny after failed uprisings. In this way, America could "feed and nourish the flame of freedom."[4]

In her 1852 Paine speech, Rose urged the American government to intervene to prevent Russian encroachment in Europe and to support democracy throughout the continent:

> Non-intervention!—There is no such thing as non-intervention . . . Silence is consent; and silence, where life and liberty [are] at stake, where—by a timely protest, we could stay the destroyer's hand, and not to do so, is as criminal as giving actual aid to the oppressor, for it answers his purpose; he can achieve the foul deed. . . . What kind of aid does the Czar of Russia require to crush freedom in Europe? Precisely such as England and this country give him—a

passive consent to his active intervention, in violation of the laws of nations as well as of humanity.

Recalling the devastation caused by war and despotism in her native country, Rose felt that timely intervention against oppressors could serve as a deterrent to prevent future wars and to preserve freedom and peace. She said of Poland: "Had intervention . . . existed before the crowned pirates plundered and divided Poland, peace might have been there." With words as relevant to the twentieth and twenty-first centuries as they were to the nineteenth century, Rose reminded listeners that peace cannot exist when freedom is crushed: "Peace! What a mockery! Cry peace in Russia, Austria, France, Italy and Germany, to the tens of thousands immured in living tombs, whose silence is broken only by the clanking of the chains that corrode their limbs!"[5]

The *Boston Investigator* called Rose's 1852 Paine speech "admirable" and "eloquent." Several Ohio newspapers praised her oratory gifts and gave lengthy excerpts from her speech, calling it "spirited" and "truly forcible."[6]

Rose was addressing audiences in a nation that was increasingly xenophobic. A New York-based political party popular in the 1850's, the American Party, known as the "Know-Nothings," aimed to eliminate all foreigners and Catholics from public office, impose a twenty-one-year residency requirement for naturalization, deport foreign paupers and criminals and ban the use of foreign languages from schools and public documents.[7] Rose made a scathing reference to this party in another Paine speech, saying that there are some minds "so thoroughly 'Know-Nothing' as to be ignorant that human rights recognize no sex, country or color.—It is easier to win a battle than to conquer minds filled with Know-Nothingism . . . It is much easier to take a fortress, composed even of granite, than to storm a citadel of prejudice sanctified by superstition, engrafted by age and strengthened by habit . . . "

Turning to the topic of the Crimean War, fought between Russia and the Allied forces of the United Kingdom, France, Sardinia and the Ottoman Empire in 1853–1856, Rose emphasized that moral battles could be as challenging as physical ones: "While the inroads the Allied armies make on the walls of Sebastopol are constantly . . . repaired by the enemy, the breaks and inroads we make on the stronghold of conservatism, ignorance and error can never again be repaired."[8]

Long before the first women's rights convention at Seneca Falls, New York, in 1848, women's rights advocates had begun voicing protests in Europe. During the French Revolution, Olympe de Gouges published her pamphlet, *Declaration of the Rights of Woman and of the Female Citizen* (1791) in answer to the *Declaration of the Rights of Man and of the Citizen* (1789). An Englishwoman, Mary Wollstonecraft, published *A Vindication of the Rights of Woman* (1792), a precursor to the reform ideas of Scottish-born

Frances Wright. These activists all advocated women's educational, political and social rights. During the 1848 Revolution in France, novelist George Sand (Aurore Dupin) began publishing her own newspaper, expressing support for women's rights.

From the First National Woman's Rights Convention to the last meeting of the American Equal Rights Association in 1869, Rose often spoke of the global significance of women's rights. "We are not contending here for the rights of women of New England or of old England, but of the world," she proclaimed in 1850.[9]

Rose opened her speech at the Second National Woman's Rights Convention in 1851 by linking women's struggle for rights in America with that in France. The Revolution of 1848 had failed to bring democracy to France. Louis-Napoléon Bonaparte, elected President, would soon carry out a *coup d'état* in December 1851 and become Emperor Napoleon III, installing a repressive, authoritarian regime. Rose referenced the ominous developments unfolding in France: "Alas! Poor France! Where is thy glory? Where the glory of the Revolution of 1848, in which shone forth the pure and magnanimous spirit of an oppressed nation, struggling for Freedom? Where the fruits of that victory that gave to the world the motto, 'Liberty, Equality, and Fraternity?'"[10]

At the 1851 convention, Rose heard a letter of solidarity read aloud from Jeanne Deroin and Pauline Roland, two French feminist activists imprisoned for six months at St. Lazare prison in Paris for daring to claim equal rights with men. Deroin had tried to run as a candidate for the Legislative Assembly while Roland had twice attempted to vote. The two women wrote from their prison cell to American women's rights activists: "In France, the Re-action has suppressed the cry of Liberty of the Women of the future, deprived, like their brothers, of the [sic] Democracy, of the right to civil and political equality . . . " The women expressed their belief that socialism would provide a foundation for a more egalitarian society:

> We have . . . the profound conviction that only by the power of association, based on solidarity—by the union of the working classes of both sexes to organize labor—can be acquired completely and pacifically the Civil and Political Equality of Woman and the social rights for all.[11]

Jeanne Deroin was an outspoken journalist whose name became synonymous with the French struggle for women's rights. In one of her articles published shortly after the 1848 Revolution had established universal manhood suffrage, Deroin wrote: "Liberty, equality and fraternity are proclaimed for all. Why give women only duties without giving them the rights of citizens? If women were capable of paying taxes they should be considered fit to take part in meeting public responsibilities." Charged with "political conspiracy," Deroin was arrested in 1850 and given a six-month prison sentence. After her release from prison, Deroin would go into voluntary exile in London and would support herself with difficulty as a widow raising two children. Deroin would die in London in 1894, having spent almost half of her life in exile.[12]

Pauline Roland, a journalist and teacher, after serving six months in prison for attempting to vote, would choose to not go into exile like Jeanne Deroin. Instead, she would join a Parisian resistance movement opposed to Louis-Napoléon's *coup d'état*. Rearrested and sentenced to hard labor in a penal colony in Algeria, she would write in a letter from prison that America was a place where progressive ideas might take root: "The Puritans of the seventeenth century founded, on the other side of the Atlantic, civil, political and religious liberties, and our brothers there will sow the holy seed of Equality and Fraternity . . . " Roland, weakened from harsh prison conditions, would die at the age of 47 on a boat returning her to France.[13]

Rose spoke at the 1851 convention of parallels between the suppression of women's freedom in France and in America, implying that by failing to live up to its principles, America was a democracy in name only: "Need we wonder that France . . . does not recognize the rights of humanity in the recognition of the Rights of Woman, when even here, in this far-famed land of freedom, under a Republic that has inscribed on its banner the great truth that all men are created free and equal . . . even here . . . woman . . . has yet to plead for her rights, nay, for her life . . . ?"[14]

How did Jeanne Deroin and Pauline Roland hear about the American women's rights movement? According to historian Carol Faulkner, news of the women's rights conventions had traveled across the Atlantic through newspapers such as the *New York Tribune* and through essays such as "Enfranchisement of Women," published by British feminist Harriet Taylor Mill, wife of the philosopher John Stuart Mill. These progressive movements in America had captured the attention of European reformers.[15]

This story of the two French activists, Jeanne Deroin and Pauline Roland, illustrates the tragic consequences for protesters in France during the regime of Louis-Napoléon. After Rose's speech on behalf of these women at the convention, she would later meet with Jeanne Deroin in London[16] and would again speak of her plight and that of other French women's rights activists at the 1856 Seventh National Woman's Rights Convention:

> Madame Roland was imprisoned for uttering the truth, in consequence of which imprisonment she lost her arm. Jeanne Deroin was exiled, and now resides in London, where she supports herself and her two daughters. She was educating them herself, because she had no means to pay for their education. She filled

their minds with noble thoughts and feelings, even to the very sacrifice of themselves for the benefit of the race.[17]

Rose denounced the despotism of Napoléon III and offered a resolution, later passed, "in support of the cause of women in Paris, the worthy successors of Pauline Roland and Jeanne Deroin, who in the face of imperial despotism, dare to tell the truth." She excoriated the French government for its human rights violations: "The usurper that now disgraces the throne, as well as the name he bears, does not allow the free utterance of a single free thought. Men and women are taken up privately and imprisoned, and no newspaper dared to publish any account of it."[18]

Internationalism, xenophobia and racism all took center stage at the New York State Woman's Rights Convention in September 1853, later dubbed the "Mob Convention." Gangs of rowdies disrupted speeches throughout the afternoon and evening, often preventing speakers from being heard. The sixty-year-old abolitionist and women's rights advocate, Sojourner Truth, facing racist jeers, rebuked the crowd for "hissing like snakes and geese": "We've all been trampled down, so nobody thought we'd ever get up again. But we have come up and I'm here. . . . You may hiss as much as you please, but you can't stop it [women's rights]; it's bound to come."[19]

Rose introduced Mathilde Franziska Anneke at this convention. Anneke had fought alongside her husband Fritz during the failed 1848 uprising in Germany. An American immigrant, she had become a renowned women's rights advocate and author, and had started the first women's rights newspaper published by a woman, *Deutsche Frauen-Zeitung* (German Woman's Newspaper).[20] Rose, who was fluent in German, served as a translator for Anneke at the convention. Anneke's presence on the podium and her speech in German stirred the crowd's deep anti-immigrant and anti-German feelings. According to the *New York Express,* Rose "preserved the utmost calmness during the uproar."

As Anneke attempted to speak, gangs of hooligans began hissing, shouting and shrieking, drowning out her voice. Anneke was comparing the political situation in Germany with that in America: "On the other side of the Atlantic there is no freedom of any kind and we have not even the right to claim freedom of speech. But can it be that here, too, there are tyrants who violate [the] individual right to express our opinions on any subject? And do you call yourselves republicans? No, there is no republic without freedom of speech." Wendell Phillips, renowned abolitionist and orator, attempted to quell the disturbance: "You are looking upon one who has faced the cannon of Francis Joseph [emperor of Austria-Hungary], fighting bravely for the liberty of the people." Rose mounted the podium, saying: "I call upon the police . . . to preserve order. As citizens of New York we have a right to this protection."[21]

The police did not intercede and as jeers overwhelmed the speakers' voices, Rose reluctantly adjourned the meeting.

"I surrendered with the courageous band of my comrades-in-arms," Anneke would later recall, "and we quickly left the tabernacle." Years later, writing of her long career as a public speaker, Anneke would recall that "Mob Convention": "My voice was overwhelmed by the sound of sneers, scoffs and hisses . . . Then, through the support of our friends Ernestine Rose and Wendell Phillips, who are ever ready in the cause of human rights, I was allowed in my native tongue to echo . . . the cry for justice and freedom."[22] Anneke would lecture on women's rights in many Eastern cities in America before moving to Milwaukee, where she would teach at a school for girls. Rose and Anneke became close friends and allies.

Ernestine Rose was ill for much of 1856 with an "inflammation of the lungs," and she and her husband hoped that a sea voyage and six-month vacation in Europe would restore her health. She wrote in a farewell letter to the *Boston Investigator* that they hoped to visit England, France, Germany and Italy. "After twenty years as a volunteer soldier in the cause of Truth," she wrote, "I should be permitted a furlough . . . to gather fresh strength . . . " She mentioned wanting to visit Poland as well: "Whether I shall be able once more to see my own poor native land, I know not; nor could it be much gratification to me, except that I could find it in a happier condition, or could be instrumental in placing it in one."[23] Nearly thirty years away from her native land, Rose maintained her strong identification with her Polish roots, and this informed her views on human rights.

Rose's travel letters, published in the *Boston Investigator* over the course of her six-month European trip, reflected her views on social conditions in England, France and Italy, and expressed her opinions on human rights and social reforms. In her first letter, published on July 30, 1856, Rose wrote of her seasickness for much of the five-week-voyage on a packet ship. Despite her improved physical state when the ocean was tranquil, Rose was not happy with the quiet sea, as she explained:

> The ocean in a calm looks to me like a nation which by long and unsuccessful attempts to free itself from the iron yoke of despotism, has subsided into apathy and inaction, which is like the calm of death, and which will require the raging of a tempest to call it again into life. I prefer the breezes to blow and the sea to be in motion. . . . The billows . . . soon rise to the surface crowned with the beautiful silver-crested foam, which, like moral greatness in man, can be obtained only by contact with each other.

She saw the sea as a metaphor for society. As a social reformer, she preferred agitation to tranquility, since "a dead calm . . . is conservative, anti-progressive. In it there is no health, no hope, no life."[24]

A few weeks after their arrival in London, the Roses visited Robert Owen, now eighty-six years old. She described him in a letter to the *Boston Investigator*: "We found him in excellent health and spirits. He writes, walks and rides every day . . . He is very remarkable for his age; still we could see quite a change in him." In addition to observing physical changes, Rose noticed an important change in his philosophy. Whereas for most of his life he had rejected religion, he was now enamored of Spiritualism—a belief that spirits of the dead have the ability to communicate with the living. Rose noted: "On Spiritualism he is as earnest and enthusiastic as his truthful and warm nature has been on any subject . . . It is needless to say, that his endeavors to convince me *into* it, and mine to convince him *out* of it, met with equal success." She resisted his efforts to influence her thinking, just as she had rejected her father's religious views long ago. Rose would remain firm in her convictions. Her constancy and refusal to compromise on her secular humanist beliefs were both a source of pride and a liability for Rose, putting her at odds with conservative Christian society in America.[25]

In her letter from London, Rose commented that women were not admitted to the Houses of Parliament unless they obtained in advance a permit. In addition, they were confined to a tiny gallery, "enclosed in the front by a close metal wire-work, like that of a prison window, which allows you to look through only with one eye at a time." Despite Great Britain's policy of restricting women's access to the Houses of Parliament, Rose, through her determination, succeeded in entering the gallery without a permit and listening to a debate at the House of Commons.[26]

Rose remarked that there were many "castes" and "grades" in English society and that "each grade looked down with contempt on all those beneath, and [looked] with slavish subservience on those above it." Reform movements were "sound asleep," according to Rose, but in her conversations with British women, she learned about petitions to improve laws for married women that had been presented to Parliament but not yet acted upon. "We can do nothing with the present Parliament," her British friend had told her. Rose observed: "Everything here is slow and heavy; it requires time—long, long time to move or change anything (except the weather)."[27]

Rose's visit to the Tower of London showed her the cruelty of rulers with absolute authority: "In the White Tower is the dungeon where the two children of Edward IV were stifled, and the dark cell where Sir Walter Raleigh was incarcerated for thirteen years." She seemed as much disturbed by the barbarism of authoritarian rulers from distant centuries as from recent times. Visiting a large room in the Tower of London, Rose identified with the sufferings of all those who had been incarcerated there. She saw "walls covered with the names, dates and last sentiments, graven with the agony of death, as a legacy to and a protest from the spirit of humanity. In an underground dungeon, 600 Jews were incarcerated at one time."[28] Throughout her career as an activist, Rose would speak out against authoritarianism in Europe and in the United States.

Writing about her travels in Italy, Rose bemoaned "poor degraded Rome . . . whose past greatness proclaims louder and places in still bolder relief its present shame. . . . The roads from Florence to Rome, and from Rome to Naples are infested by beggars, brigands and priests." She decried the wealth and power of the Church, which "directs [beggars and brigands] to some other life; otherwise they might not so willingly submit to their miserable condition in this [one] . . . " In Rose's opinion, the priests played a disturbing role: "to give the brigands absolution (with a free license for their trade)."

As a freethinker, Rose saw religion as a menace to progress. She believed that it distracted people from the task of building a more just society by focusing their attention on an afterlife. She could not appreciate Italy's beautiful climate and scenery because of her preoccupation with the social inequities, crime and corruption that she witnessed: "*Lazzaroni* [idlers, beggars or persons who subsist on odd jobs] are in the daily pay of a miserable pittance from the King, to be ready at his bidding to massacre and plunder the better portion of the people."[29]

She wrote at length from France but could not mail her letters until she had left this country because of repressive censorship laws under Napoléon III. Rose felt a strong kinship with French people. In other countries, according to Rose, the barriers between educated and uneducated, wealthy and poor could not be overcome but in France, Rose found, "there is no overwhelming pride in the rich and learned; no slavish humility in the poor and ignorant . . . They mix together, treat each other with becoming respect and fraternal civility."[30]

Wherever she traveled, her thoughts led her to the subject of social reform. After visiting Père Lachaise Cemetery in Paris, she wrote: "There are many fine monuments but I did not like to stay long in this confined city of the dead. It reminded me too much of the miserable condition of many cities of the living."[31] She visited a Gobelins tapestry factory and marveled at magnificent tapestries whose colors were "as fresh as new." Some dated back to the seventeenth century. "I looked at [them] with intense admiration," she wrote, "but I felt the greatest interest in the artisans weaving the tapestries. They are a fine, noble, intellectual set of men." She spoke with several of them. One man told her that he had spent eleven years working on one tapestry. What made a strong impression on her was that these artisans received very low wages. "The best [got] only 2500f, or 500 dollars a year," she wrote. According to one weaver, "an increase in wages [was] under consideration."[32]

As a social reformer and human rights activist, Rose's focus was always on the lives of ordinary men and women. She cared far more about improving living conditions than about memorializing the dead or admiring works of art. Rose was shocked at the changes she witnessed in Paris since her previous visit twenty-six years earlier. The effects of despotism were visible everywhere. "Paris, with all her beauties . . . is at present little less than one vast barrack . . . The city is full of soldiers . . . Nor is this the worst . . . There is a much more formidable army, an *espionnage* [spy network] against which you cannot guard except by a dead silence on all subjects connected with freedom . . . Paris is as still as the grave." The French government had banned all discussions of politics, strictly censored newspapers and books, particularly those related to the subject of women's rights, and imprisoned many dissidents. In the United States, social reformers like Rose had to contend with unruly audiences and hecklers, while French reformers of the mid-nineteenth century might have to pay for their protests with their lives.

Rose's fluency in French enabled her to speak with dissidents, writers and social reformers in France. Unable to publish their progressive articles and books in their homeland, they managed to have them published in Belgium or Italy and then smuggled into France. Rose became a link between European and American activists, publicizing their ideas and informing them about progress made towards human rights in the United States. One important contact Rose made in France was with Jenny d'Héricourt, a practitioner of homeopathic medicine, certified midwife, feminist journalist and writer who helped to organize workers' associations. Rose wrote of her: "Madame d'Héricourt is a physician, a woman of noble character, great energy and talents; she is a thorough reformer, particularly for women's rights and against priests and churches; she writes a great deal but no journal in Paris dare[s to] publish her articles, so she has them published in Sardinia . . . and brought to Paris."[33]

Until about thirty years ago, very little was known about Jenny d'Héricourt, since she left no diary or correspondence. This changed when a scholar found her thinly disguised autobiography in an 1869 American newspaper. We now know that d'Héricourt spearheaded much of women's political activity in Paris during the 1848 Revolution, created two short-lived newspapers, wrote a book on women's rights, *La Femme affranchie* (The Liberated Woman), published a short biography of Ernestine Rose and helped to organize an international association called the "Universal Woman's League for Woman's Rights and Universal Peace."[34] D'Héricourt moved to Chicago in 1863 and stayed there for ten years, where she continued to lecture on women's rights at American conventions and to facilitate connections between American and French activists. French reformers like d'Héricourt were thus able to continue their advocacy of women's rights despite the threat of harsh punishment during Napoleon III's regime.

Another noteworthy immigrant and acquaintance of Ernestine Rose was Ottilie Assing. An abolitionist and journalist born in Germany, Assing wrote for a German-American newspaper, the *Morgenblatt für gebildete Leser* (Morning Paper for Educated Readers). She became acquainted with Frederick Douglass in 1856 when she interviewed him for her newspaper. They would have a twenty-eight-year romantic relationship. Assing translated his works into German, assisted him with his abolitionist writings and attended conventions with him.[35]

Ottilie Assing met Ernestine Rose at a women's rights convention in 1858 and wrote of her: "Her opinions are based on a clear, liberal conception of all things and are not hemmed in by tradition. Her speeches . . . reveal a broadly educated, independent and lucid mind; nothing is murky, nebulous or illogical."[36] Assing supported equal rights and equality of opportunity for women and men but had little respect for some in the American women's movement because she found their "bloomer" costumes extreme and some of their behavior eccentric. She felt that this exposed them to ridicule.[37]

Assing distinguished Rose from other women's rights activists in this way:

[Rose's] knowledge of two continents has broadened her horizons; experience and understanding have matured her opinion . . . It takes women like Ernestine Rose, a woman of education, experience, dignity, i.e., professional women with expertise and devoid of the eccentric, to lead the way to a free womanhood. Only then would the 'baroque' appearance [of some activists] give way to more substantial accomplishments than any refusal to pay taxes or any penchant for sermonizing can ever achieve.[38]

It was Rose's European background, education and internationalism, Assing argued, that gave her the maturity and experience necessary to advance the cause of women's rights.

During the decades that followed, Rose continued to speak out about political events occurring in Europe. In a letter to a newspaper editor, she expressed her outrage at the British divorce bill passed in 1857 which denied all rights to women: "I must say, that as low as my estimate has ever been of . . . statesmen and legislators who enact laws in defiance of human rights which recognize no sex, it falls far short of the utter contempt if not abhorrence . . . which [the divorce bill has] inspired . . . "[39]

She publicly expressed her shock and anger at the kidnapping of a six-year-old Jewish child in Bologna, Italy—Edgardo Mortara—seized by agents of Pope Pius IX after a servant had secretly baptized him. In the eyes of the Church, the boy's involuntary baptism was enough to make him a

Catholic and required that he be permanently removed from his Jewish family. International pleas for his return, including those of Napoléon III, fell on deaf ears in the Vatican. Edgardo Mortara would grow up separated from his family and would eventually become a priest.

The Mortara Affair was very disturbing for Rose. It was a human rights violation and an extreme example of religious fanaticism and anti-Semitism. As a European Jew, she undoubtedly identified with the Mortara family. Rose excoriated the Vatican kidnappers in her Paine speech in 1859: "[In] Rome, in the name of religion and of God, bands of ecclesiastical marauders break in at the dead of night to rob parents of their children—as in the case of Mortara . . . "[40] She again spoke of Mortara two years later: "Rome . . . is still in the fiendish grasp of spiritual tyrants, more corrupt and implacable than all others, whose spare time from heavenly affairs is spent in stealing children from their parents."[41] Although Rose had broken off her ties with organized religion, she staunchly defended Jewish rights and spoke out vehemently against anti-Semitism, just as she had always defended all human rights.[42]

The Mortara Affair had international repercussions and it galvanized the world Jewish community. In the United States, it led to the creation of the Board of Delegates of American Israelites in 1859, to protect Jewish civil and religious rights at home and abroad. In France, it was a motivating factor in the formation of the *Alliance Israélite Universelle* (Universal Jewish Alliance), a prominent organization dedicated to safeguarding the human rights of Jews around the world. This organization continues to exist in the twenty-first century.[43]

In her 1860 Paine speech, Rose rejoiced over good international news in several countries: a revolutionary leader, Giuseppe Garibaldi, had helped to unite Italy; Russia had given freedom to the serfs; and Louis-Napoléon, "usurper of an Emperor's throne of '52," had proclaimed himself the champion of freedom in Italy and had "relaxed his iron grasp from the throat of subjugated France, [giving] her back a part of the rights he [had] so basely deprived her of." Rose hoped that Napoléon would soon "return the rest [of France's rights] or lose all."[44]

After the construction of the first transatlantic telegraph lines in the 1860's, better communications and transnational print culture would help activists to form international human rights movements. Even at the contentious last meeting of the American Equal Rights Association in 1869, which marked a split in the women's rights movement over the issue of the Fifteenth Amendment, Rose noted that they had achieved success in creating an international movement. She commented on the number of American and European guest speakers participating in the association: "The world moves! We need not seek further than this convention assembled here tonight to show that it moves. We have assembled here delegates from the East and the West, from the North and the South, from all over the United States, from England, France and from Germany."

Mathilde Anneke spoke at this meeting about the welcome she was now receiving at her lectures: "Today [the public] greets us with deferent respect. Such giant steps are made by public opinion! . . . Such an expression of sentiment is to us the most certain and joyful token of a gigantic revolution in public opinion . . . " Jenny d'Héricourt also spoke at this meeting, calling for a series of resolutions for the creation of a "league of all women claiming rights in America and Europe."[45]

William and Ernestine Rose moved to Europe in June 1869 to restore Ernestine Rose's health by a rest and a complete change of air. They stayed for some time in Luxeuil-les-Bains, in Burgundy, France, at a health spa. It was "the most curious and interesting town I have ever seen," Rose wrote. Her health improved from "its various springs of hot and cold waters." Even in this remote region of Burgundy, Rose met some Europeans who "knew my name and heretical proclivities, which gave rise to very interesting conversations . . . on religion and women's rights."[46]

Both in America and Europe, Ernestine Rose would continue to use her international platform to speak of her ideal of a democratic society founded on the principle of natural rights, of inherent human rights. As an internationalist and an "outsider," she was able to go beyond American partisan politics to reach a wider, global audience. While many of America's promises would continue to remain unfulfilled in the nineteenth century and beyond, Rose and other activists had planted seeds of change and had begun to see their fruition at home and abroad.

NOTES

1. James S. Pula, "'The Noblest Deed in a Hundred Years': Polish Participation in the Antislavery Crusade," *Polish American Studies* 75, no. 1 (Champaign: University of Illinois Press, Spring 2018):1–8.

2. Ernestine L. Rose, "Speeches at the Seventh National Woman's Rights Convention," November 26, 1856, in Doress-Worters, ed., *Mistress of Herself: Speeches and Letters of Ernestine L. Rose, Early Women's Rights Leader* (New York: The Feminist Press, 2008), 228.

3. Ernestine L. Rose, "Speech at the Thomas Paine Celebration," January 29, 1849, in Doress-Worters, 73.

4. Ernestine L. Rose, "Speech at the Thomas Paine Celebration," January 29, 1850, in Doress-Worters, 77–78.

5. Ernestine L. Rose, "Speech at Paine Celebration,"*Boston Investigator*, February 11, 1852, 1.

6. Ernestine L. Rose, "Multiple News Items," *Boston Investigator*, March 3, 1852, 1.

7. Edwin G. Burrows and Mike Wallace, *Gotham: A History of New York City to 1898* (New York: Oxford University Press, 1999), 829.

8. Ernestine L. Rose, "Speech at the Thomas Paine Celebration," January 29, 1855, in Doress-Worters, 182–183.

9. Ernestine L. Rose, "Speech at the First National Woman's Rights Convention," October 23–24, 1850, *New York Tribune*, October 25, 1850, in Doress-Worters, 47.

10. Ernestine L. Rose, "Speech at the Second National Woman's Rights Convention," October 15–16, 1851, in Doress-Worters, 91–92.

11. Pauline Roland and Jeanne Deroin, "Letter from Two Women's Rights Reformers," June 15, 1851, St. Lazare Prison, Paris, in Doress-Worters, 87–90.

12. Joyce Dixon-Fyle, *Female Writers' Struggle for Rights and Education for Women in France (1848–1871)* (New York: Lang, 2006), 16–18.

13. Pauline Roland, Letter of April 15, 1852, in "The Death of Pauline Roland," *The Una,* November 1, 1853, 165. For more on Pauline Roland (1805–1852), see Dixon-Fyle, 54–55, 75–78.

14. Doress-Worters, 90–92.

15. Carol Faulkner, "How Did an International Agenda Shape the American Women's Rights Movement, 1840–1869?" September 2012, Schlesinger Library, Radcliffe Institute, Harvard University, ProQuest Ebrary.

16. Bonnie S. Anderson, *The Rabbi's Atheist Daughter: Ernestine Rose, International Feminist Pioneer* (New York: Oxford University Press, 2017), 104.

17. Ernestine L. Rose, "Speech at the Seventh National Woman's Rights Convention," November 26, 1856, in Doress-Worters, 224–225.

18. Doress-Worters, 224–225.

19. Sojourner Truth, quoted in "Woman's Rights Convention," *Cleveland Daily Herald*, September 9, 1853, 1.

20. For more on Mathilde Anneke, see Ellen Engseth, "Mathilde Franziska Anneke," *Encyclopedia of Milwaukee,* https://www.emke.uwm.edu/entry/mathilde-franziska-anneke.

21. Ernestine L. Rose and Mathilde Franziska Anneke, "Speeches at the New York State Woman's Rights Convention," September 9, 1853, in Doress-Worters, 155–156.

22. Ernestine L. Rose is mentioned in the *New York Express* and in *The Liberator*, September 16, 1853, 4; Mathilde Anneke is quoted in Elizabeth Cady Stanton, Susan B. Anthony, Matilda Joslyn Gage, eds., *History of Woman Suffrage*, vol. 2:392–393, Gutenberg E-book.

23. Ernestine L. Rose, "Letter to the Editor," *Boston Investigator*, May 5, 1856, in Doress-Worters, 207–210.

24. Ernestine L. Rose, "Travel Letter No. 1," *Boston Investigator*, July 30, 1856, 1.

25. Ernestine L. Rose, "Travel Letter No. 2," London, July 6, 1856, in Doress-Worters, 211–212.

26. Ibid.

27. Ernestine L. Rose, "Travel Letter No. 4," London, *Boston Investigator*, August 20, 1856, 1.

28. Ernestine L. Rose, "Travel Letter No. 3," London, July 13, 1856, in Doress-Worters, 214.

29. Ernestine L. Rose, "Travel Letter No. 11," Italy, October 20, 1856, in Doress-Worters, 219–220.

30. Ernestine L. Rose, "Travel Letter No. 10," Berlin, September 30, 1856, in Doress-Worters, 216–217.

31. Ernestine L. Rose, "Travel Letter No. 8," Berlin, *Boston Investigator*, November 19, 1856, 1.

32. Ernestine L. Rose, "Travel Letter No. 7," Berlin, *Boston Investigator*, October 29, 1856, 1.

33. Ernestine L. Rose, "Travel Letter No. 9," Berlin, *Boston Investigator*, November 26, 1856, 1.

34. Karen Offen, "A Nineteenth-Century French Feminist Rediscovered: Jenny d'Héricourt, 1809–1875," *Signs* 13, no. 1 (Fall 1987): 144, ProQuest.

35. Maria Diedrich, *Love Across Color Lines: Ottilie Assing and Frederick Douglass* (New York: Hill and Wang, 1999).

36. Diedrich, 103.

37. Diedrich, 209. "Bloomers" were a knee-length dress worn over loose-fitting trousers, to give women more freedom of movement. Amelia Bloomer, an American women's rights advocate, popularized them in the 1850's. Elizabeth Cady Stanton wore this outfit, while Ernestine Rose wore more traditional dresses. The term became a synonym for a women's rights activist.

38. Diedrich, 103, 209.

39. Ernestine L. Rose, "Letter to the Editor," *Boston Investigator,* October 3, 1857, in Doress-Worters, 238–239.

40. Ernestine L. Rose, "Speech at the Thomas Paine Celebration," January 31, 1859, in Doress-Worters, 247.

41. Ernestine L. Rose, "Speech at the Thomas Paine Celebration," January 29, 1861, in Doress-Worters, 291–292.

42. See also Rose's defense of American Jews in her 1863 debate with Horace Seaver: "Ernestine L. Rose and Horace Seaver, Debate on the Jews in the *Boston Investigator*, October 28, 1863 to April 13, 1864," in Doress-Worters, 311–333. I will discuss this subject in detail in Chapter 6.

43. David I. Kertzer, *The Kidnapping of Edgardo Mortara* (New York: Vintage Books, 1998).

44. Ernestine L. Rose, "Speech at the Thomas Paine Celebration," January 29, 1861, in Doress-Worters, 291–292.

45. Ernestine L. Rose, Mathilde Anneke and Jenny d'Héricourt are quoted in Stanton, Anthony, Gage, eds., *History of Woman Suffrage*, vol. 2: 393–396.

46. Ernestine L. Rose, "Letter," *Boston Investigator*, September 15, 1869, 2.

Chapter 6

Climbing a Mountain

Freethought and Religious Freedom

As a secular reformer in nineteenth-century America, Ernestine Rose fought for social justice and equality while facing deep hostility and resistance to change. She endured rage, indignation and threats of tar and feathering for speaking out against slavery and she was shouted down for her advocacy of women's rights. Yet it was Rose's proud devotion to the cause of freethought that made her an outcast even among some liberal reformers. Rose was one of a very small number of activists who sought to build a movement for social change without any reference to religion. She faced some of her harshest opposition to the cause of freethought.

The United States was a largely conservative Protestant country that experienced its second "Great Awakening" of religious fervor led by evangelical ministers during the first half of the nineteenth century. Preachers fostered in their congregants a sense of personal guilt and a need for salvation; they portrayed freethought and atheism as dangerous and immoral. In this social climate, Rose's passion for reason and for the freedom to be irreligious—to be an "infidel" in the language of her day—was enough to alienate all those who defined respectability. She proudly accepted this "infidel" label, even as it hurt her success and brought her much negative publicity in the press.

Many abolitionists and women's rights advocates shunned Rose for her rejection of religious authority. The Declaration of Independence rather than the Bible was her foundational document, a risky position for her to take. Abner Kneeland, founder of the first American freethought newspaper, *The Boston Investigator*, was indicted and convicted on the charge of blasphemy, for having made an equivocal statement about God's existence. He served sixty days in prison.[1] One of Rose's good friends in the Owenite freethought community, George Holyoake, a British newspaper editor, served six months in prison for this same crime of blasphemy.[2]

Freethought was not a new concept in the nineteenth century. It has existed for centuries. During the period of the Enlightenment in Europe, scientists and philosophers, including John Locke, Jean-Jacques Rousseau, Denis Diderot and Voltaire, argued that reason and human experience, rather than religious dogma, determined the validity of all beliefs. Freethinkers throughout history have shared this perspective: they have formed their opinions independently of any tradition or authority. They represent diverse points of view, identifying themselves as atheists, agnostics, rationalists, secular humanists or deists. The Founding Fathers in America were influenced by reason-centered Enlightenment thought and wrote the Constitution without any reference to God.[3] Many Founding Fathers, including Thomas Jefferson, Benjamin Franklin and Thomas Paine, considered themselves to be deists or rationalists. They stood for rational inquiry, skepticism about religious dogma, and religious tolerance. Thomas Jefferson wrote of "building a wall of separation between Church and State," when he referred to the First Amendment.[4]

Even as the foundations of the world's first secular constitution were being laid, growing tensions in America between rationalists and evangelical Christians posed a threat to religious freedom. During ratification debates in 1787 for the Constitution, one speaker at the Massachusetts convention warned that unless the chief executive was required to take a religious oath, "a Turk, a Jew, a Roman Catholic, and what is worse than all, a Universalist, may be President of the United States."[5] President George Washington's 1790 letter to the Jewish community of Newport, Rhode Island was a powerful affirmation of the principles of religious freedom and freedom of conscience:

> All possess alike liberty of conscience and immunity of citizenship. It is now no more that toleration is spoken of as if it were the indulgence of one class of people that another enjoyed the exercise of their inherent natural rights, for, happily, the Government of the United States, which gives to bigotry no sanction, to persecution no assistance, requires only that they who live under its protection should demean themselves as good citizens.[6]

The Constitution guarantees the right to religious and intellectual freedom, and prohibits religious tests for public office. The First Amendment declares: "Congress shall make no law respecting an establishment of religion, or prohibiting the free exercise thereof . . . " Although this nation has clearly defended the principle of secularism, throughout our history there have been fierce controversies about this subject. Further complicating this issue of secularism was the fact that states were free to pass their own laws regarding relations between church and state. Massachusetts didn't strike out all religious restrictions for its laws until 1833 and Connecticut withheld equal rights for Jews for another ten years.[7] The governor of South Carolina issued a Thanksgiving Day proclamation in 1844 that offended non-Christians and provoked letters of protest when it offered prayers specifically mentioning Jesus Christ. After repeated public protests by Jewish citizens, the succeeding governor resolved the controversy by issuing a nonsectarian proclamation.[8]

While the Constitution established separation of church and state, the "Great Awakening" spread religious fervor and rejected secularism. Tensions between these two opposing beliefs would continue through much of the nineteenth century, stirring acrimonious debate.

Rose's activism for freethought and religious freedom had its roots in her early experiences living in Poland. By introducing herself to the American public as "a daughter of poor, crushed Poland, and the down-trodden and persecuted people called the Jews,"[9] Rose was suggesting that her origins, growing up in a country in which Jews were denied equal rights and subjected to persecution, had given her unique insight into oppression and had helped her to become a strong advocate for religious freedom and social change.

As an activist who exemplified Jewish ethical values, Rose was a forerunner of many early twentieth-century social reformers such as Lillian Wald, Maud Nathan and Rose Schneiderman, as well as later women's rights advocates such as Bella Abzug and Betty Friedan.[10] She never converted out of Judaism and although she rejected all organized religion, she was quick to defend the Jewish people when they were attacked and to forcefully protest against anti-Semitism. As shown in Chapter 1, from her Jewish upbringing and education she had learned to argue forcefully on matters of ethical principles and to follow the Judaic ethic of repairing the world. Even as a secularist, Rose was not indifferent to religion. She often engaged in spirited debates on interpretations of biblical passages.[11]

When Rose rebelled at age sixteen against an arranged marriage and against the constraints of Orthodox Judaism, she took her first bold action on behalf of religious freedom. Her realization that religion limited and confined people's lives, particularly women's lives, would stay with her for the rest of her life. Her assertion of intellectual and religious freedom placed her in the tradition of other "non-Jewish Jews," from Spinoza to Marx, Freud and Trotsky, who went beyond the boundaries of Judaism, and in so doing helped to bring about important new social, political, philosophical and psychological movements. It was perhaps because Rose grew up on the borderlines of various civilizations, cultures and religions, and because she absorbed these different influences and was able to rise above them, that she could "strike out mentally into wide new horizons" and become a trailblazer.[12]

As discussed in Chapter 1, after Rose left Poland she spent two years in Berlin, where she encountered Enlightenment thought. She then traveled to France, in the midst of revolutionary upheaval, and to London in 1830. Her

European experiences would inform her strong preference for republicanism and rationalism.

In England, Rose found in Owenism a secular philosophy that would guide her and influence her throughout her life. Instead of professing faith in Christianity or in any other religion, Owen put his faith in the innate goodness of mankind, believing that each person would live a virtuous and productive life if provided with a good social environment and a well-rounded, broad education. Owenism harmonized with Rose's own views opposing religious institutions. This philosophy inspired Rose to focus on urgent human concerns in the here and now, particularly on the immediate need to end slavery, racism and gender inequality.[13]

Although they considered themselves Owenites, William and Ernestine Rose supported themselves through private enterprise—with profits from William's jewelry and silversmith shop and from the sale of Ernestine Rose's perfumed paper—and they never lived in the experimental community in Skaneateles. It is paradoxical that Rose, a socialist, became famous for helping to pass the Married Women's Property Act. As a pragmatic reformer, she fought for greater equality and social justice in battles she believed she could win during her lifetime. She did not strive for a utopian society.

New York City was a center for a multitude of movements and ideologies: there were socialists, both freethinkers and church members; and there were secularists who supported separation of church and state. Rose, however, was in the smallest minority of all reformers, as an atheist freethinker and as a woman who defied social norms by speaking in public. She began her activism in support of Owen's philosophy at Tammany Hall Sunday lectures sponsored by the freethought community.[14]

Her views on religion made her appear too radical even for some of the more progressive reformers. Rose encountered fierce hostility when she began speaking in public outside the freethought community. When a crowd threatened her for daring to question a minister at a meeting, she remained calm and composed, and continued her remarks after quiet was restored. Her composure made a deep impression upon those present.[15] She was assailed by hisses and catcalls when she told her listeners at the New England Social Reform Society Convention in 1844: "[Churches]. . . . oppress you. They prevent progression. They are opposed to reason."[16] She was blatantly accusing the church of standing in the way of progress. Her refusal to compromise on her principles made her throw all caution to the wind. Rose's speeches alienated many listeners by her harsh rhetoric against religious institutions.

Why would Rose seriously harm her reputation as a reformer and risk antagonizing her audience? She gave this answer:

The secret of [many orators'] success consists in swimming with the current—in not being too far in advance of society; and so in their writings and speeches they give the people, not what they most need and ought to hear, but what would be most acceptable to the pride, vanity or interest of their hearers or readers . . . I can give no other name than ignorance, or moral cowardice, which hinders far more than it advances the progress of the [human] race.[17]

Rose spoke with blunt honesty, knowing that her lectures might alienate her listeners, because she felt that change was urgently needed in America. "Agitate! Agitate!" she would proclaim. She chose to challenge society's views on religion, for without "mental freedom"—what we today call intellectual freedom—she felt there could be no social progress.

At annual dinners commemorating Thomas Paine's birthday, Rose praised Paine both for his political contributions to the cause of American independence and for his dedication to "mental freedom." She deplored the slanderous attacks against him because of his rejection of established religion: "If the term 'religion' signifies practical virtues—justice, mercy, benevolence, charity, purity of intention, kindness of heart, devotion to truth, and an abiding love for the [human] race," Rose argued, "then Thomas Paine ought to be considered one of the most religious men that ever lived."[18] This same description might be applied to Rose herself, despite her rejection of all religious institutions.

What were Thomas Paine's religious beliefs that so shocked Americans and caused him to be vilified? He declared in his "profession of faith" in *The Age of Reason*: "I believe in one God, and no more; and I hope for happiness beyond this life. I believe in the equality of man; and I believe that religious duties consist in doing justice, loving mercy, and in endeavoring to make our fellow-creatures happy." He was one of the principal exponents of Deism, believing in a God of moral truth while not accepting the creed of any church. "My own mind is my own church," he proclaimed. His stance on rational inquiry and religious tolerance had influenced the Founding Fathers to advocate for liberal political ideals and the separation of church and state, yet he was denounced by many for rejecting organized religion.[19]

At an 1850 Paine celebration, Rose reminded listeners of Paine's life, of "his disinterested devotion to the cause of Liberty—the signal services he rendered to this country in her struggle under a foreign yoke . . . " America's struggles against a foreign despot reminded Rose of other tyrants throughout history: "Every tyrant . . . pacifies his obedient slaves with the divine right to crush Humanity." To deserve the name of friends to Thomas Paine, Rose concluded, meant "to oppose obstacles to human progression, . . . to court truth only, for it is the noblest impulse to all our actions . . . Let us work on for the emancipation of man, not only from his physical but mental bondage, and hasten the glorious time when tyranny and oppression will cease . . . "[20]

Paine's message, and that of Rose, was that indoctrination, by both religious and secular leaders, had led people to distrust the power of rational thinking and had emboldened tyrannical rulers. Rose's speech was eerily prescient, anticipating growing threats to democracy with the rise of authoritarianism and religious fundamentalism in the twentieth and twenty-first centuries.

There were in fact strong reasons to criticize religious institutions in America. When churches, synagogues and temples needed to take a bold moral stand against the institution of slavery, most remained silent. Some religious leaders were guilty of using scriptural interpretations to legitimize slavery. The Orthodox Congregational Church, then the largest and most influential ecclesiastical body of Massachusetts, issued a pastoral letter of 1837 calling upon churches to close doors against abolitionists, who had "set aside the laws of God by welcoming women to their platforms and allowing them to speak in public."[21] Rose excoriated churches for their complicity in slavery: "Look at the present crisis—[in] the South with 4,000,000 of [sic] human beings in slavery, bought and sold like brute chattels under the sanction of religion and of God, which the Reverends Van Dykes and the Raphalls of the North fully endorse."[22]

Many American churches and synagogues were shockingly passive or complicit, with regard to slavery. Quakers, formally known as the Religious Society of Friends, were to their credit the first church organization to take a collective moral stand against slavery in the United States and were prominently involved in the Underground Railroad. Religious leaders from other faiths did not assert a unified moral position on this issue. Some rabbis, including Rabbi Morris J. Raphall of New York, whom Rose mentioned in her speech, claimed that the Bible and God sanctioned human bondage. When Raphall's oration was published in the press in 1861, several Christian clergymen praised it.[23]

Rabbi David Einhorn, in sharp contrast, was outspoken in his denunciation of slavery, even though his ethical position put him in great personal danger.[24] Open rioting broke out on April 19, 1861, after Einhorn gave an antislavery sermon in Baltimore, Maryland, a slave state. For four days, anyone suspected of sharing his ideas was attacked and some people were killed. Einhorn's printing presses which had published his articles were destroyed and several homes were set afire. For his own sake and his family's sake, Einhorn was forced to flee to Philadelphia.[25]

At a time when taking a stand against slavery often meant risking one's life, Ernestine Rose, as a freethinker and a Jew, forcefully denounced this evil in her lectures, taking this message even to the Deep South. According to historian Morris Schappes, "In 1853, there was only one Jew conspicuously identified with the abolitionist movement: Ernestine L. Rose." Rabbi David Einhorn and Michael Heilprin, a Polish-Jewish abolitionist, would join her in 1855 and 1856, respectively.[26]

In both Judaism and Christianity, for much of the nineteenth and some of the twentieth century, women were relegated to a separate sphere and "protected" from full participation in religious practices and American democracy. The Congregational Church of New Hampshire, for example, enacted a statute in 1843 against women speaking or making any sound in church.[27] In this way, religious institutions silenced needed discussion about issues of social justice.

Rose spoke out boldly whenever she encountered anti-Semitism and whenever she found that religion was standing in the way of social progress. She attended two lectures in 1852, titled "Hints to a Young Woman," given by Horace Mann, a social reformer, member of Congress and one of the founders of American free public education. She was disturbed by his attack on Jews and by his appeal to religious authority as an argument against women's rights. Not intimidated by Mann's prominent position in society, Rose sharply criticized Mann's views in several letters she wrote to the *Boston Investigator.* Mann had said, "For four thousand years the Jewish women did nothing but give birth to a race of unmerciful, stiff-necked men." Rose responded sarcastically, exposing his illogic and his anti-Semitism: "Unmerciful and stiff-necked as the Jews are, they still are the authors and originators of his religion, and a Jewish woman was the mother of his Redeemer. Well, gratitude is a virtue; and seeing how corrupt the race is, it is quite refreshing to find one mother's son possessing the amiable virtue of gratitude to God's (his God's) chosen people."

As someone steeped in the Bible, Rose was able to respond to Mann's religious references with her own biblical interpretation, using "Higher Criticism"—analysis separated from theological convictions and influenced by rational thought. In another one of his lectures in this series, Mann showed that he favored traditional roles for men and women, with women limited to the domestic sphere: " . . . God created the two sexes on the division of labor," Mann argued. "As mortals are created male and female, so labor and pursuits are of a similar character . . . The greatest pride of woman should be as a good house-keeper, as a scientific cook . . . to take care of the wardrobe, and keep the buttons where they belong . . . " Rose responded mockingly: "If we are to believe the literal Bible story . . . then it would appear that God did not intend man to labor at all [in the Garden of Eden] . . . Had not Mother Eve, contrary to the command of God, eaten . . . of the glorious little apple which transformed [Adam and Eve] into rational beings, and as such made it necessary for them to labor, they would have had no labor at all—No! Not even a seat in Congress . . . "

Traditional biblical scholars have interpreted Eve's partaking of the forbidden fruit as a sin for which women were to be eternally punished by pain in childbirth and subordination to their husbands. Rose interpreted this Bible story in the opposite way: Eve brought the gift of knowledge and rationalism to mankind, making it possible for someone like Horace Mann to become a Congressman. According to Rose, there is no original sin, and women and men are equally endowed with reason. For this reason, there is no religious justification for inequality between men and women.

In her concluding comments, Rose berated Mann for praising qualities of charity without exemplifying them: "How much better would it have been if the lecturer had given the proceeds of the two lectures . . . to charity. . . . Alas! charity, like the Gospel, is not practiced by those that preach it . . . It is far easier . . . to recommend all those sublime virtues which 'God and his angels so much admire,' . . . than it is to practice them!" Rose was attacking Mann's appeal to religious authority and his hypocrisy as he tried to justify the inequality of men and women. Religion, Rose felt, was an obstacle to mankind's advancement.[28]

Rose's views on the Bible and religion brought her into conflict with Antoinette L. Brown, the first ordained female minister in the United States, at the Third National Woman's Rights Convention in 1852. Reverend Brown said in support of women's rights: "The Bible recognizes the rights, duties and privileges of Woman as a public teacher, as every way equal with those of man . . . God created the first human pair [as] equals in rights, possessions and authority."

Rose responded to her colleague by reminding her that a new law introduced in the Indiana State Constitution that would have given a married woman the right to her property was recalled by the influence of a minister. She argued: "[Because he brought] the whole force of Bible argument to bear against the right of woman to her property, it was lost . . . For my part, I see no need to appeal to any written authority, particularly when it is so obscure and indefinite as to admit of different interpretations." Rose's Jewish background led her to emphasize the importance of laws, rather than of religious beliefs, since Judaism is a religion of laws and not of creed. When it came to governing society, she saw reason as the only legitimate basis for the creation of laws. The Founding Fathers had been in agreement with her viewpoint. Rose and Brown, despite their disagreements, would continue to enjoy a cordial relationship.[29]

It was at the 1853 Hartford Bible Convention, organized to debate the validity of the Bible, that Rose used more incendiary language than she had ever used before against the Bible and religion. The audience represented diverse viewpoints. There were abolitionists like William Lloyd Garrison, a practicing Christian; former ministers turned freethinkers, theology students and other observant Christians. Her main argument, that social progress depended on people making rational, rather than religion-based decisions, was an argument that several Founding Fathers supported. Her choice of words, however, would provoke an explosion of fury.

Rose first praised Martin Luther for claiming the right of conscience and of private judgment. She went on to criticize Catholicism for not allowing this freedom of thought: "According to the Bible in the hands of the Pope, there is no freedom of opinion, no variety of sects, no private judgment. The Bible tells him [the Pope] to subject human rights, reason, and judgment to his despotic rule." Rose then gave examples of tyrants committing atrocities throughout history who found justification for their crimes in the authority of the Bible.

"The time I trust will come," Rose continued, "when the Bible, like any other book, will be subjected to the test of reason . . . and by that test either stand or fall. [The Bible] has been . . . instrumental in keeping [mankind] in ignorance, degradation and vice . . . to produce war, slavery . . . and all the evils that afflict the race . . . " Rose then uttered words that would deeply shock her listeners: "Do you wish to be free? Then you must trample the Bible, the church, and the priests under your feet."[30]

Rose later gave an account of the heated atmosphere in the lecture hall: "The hall . . . which will accommodate . . . about 1600, . . . was well filled. . . . It was crowded, every standing-place being occupied, even to the outside of the doors . . . On [that] Saturday evening, they seemed to . . . use the best and only argument at their command in favor of their Bible—namely, disturbance, confusion and riot!"[31] Garrison would later write of the disturbance that evening: "The worst and grossest of the interruptions were directed against a woman, Mrs. Ernestine Rose, of great dignity of carriage and of unusual ability. [He himself] . . . had escaped . . . with slight discourtesy."[32] Rose's attack on religion stirred up negative publicity in the press, causing her to be socially ostracized among many reformers, and making it difficult for her to rent a hall for future lectures.

She spoke with more restraint and even praised a heckler for freely expressing his views at the Seventh National Woman's Rights Convention. The heckler had criticized her for bringing "no authority from revelation or from nature" to support her claims for women's rights. She responded to the heckler:

It is true we do not go to revelations written in books, but ours is older than all books . . . ours only is the true revelation, based in nature and in life . . . Do you tell me that the Bible is against our rights? . . . Our claims do not rest on the opinions of anyone, not even on those of Paul and Peter, for they are older than [them]. Books and opinions, no matter from whom they come, if they are in opposition to human rights, are nothing but dead letters.[33]

Rose was drawing here on the Enlightenment notion that reason and human experience, not religious dogma, determine the validity of all beliefs.

Rose's 1861 Boston lecture, "A Defence of Atheism" gave a clear statement of her philosophical beliefs as a freethinker:

> If I have no faith in your religion, I have faith, unbounded, unshaken faith in the principles of right, of justice, and humanity. Whatever good you are willing to do for the sake of your God, I am full as willing to do for the sake of man . . . Whatever good you would do out of fear of punishment, or hope of reward hereafter, the Atheist would do simply because *it is* good; and *being so*, he would receive the far surer and more certain reward, springing from well-doing, which would constitute his pleasure, and promote his happiness.

Rose championed an ethical, humanistic philosophy whose goal was the betterment of mankind. Doing good and avoiding evil, according to Rose, needed no reward in an afterlife. She denounced the church for its persecution throughout history of nonbelievers and believers of different faiths, and for the harm caused by directing mankind's focus toward an afterlife and away from the urgent need to alleviate poverty, injustice and inequality in our world.

As a rationalist thinker, Rose praised advances in science and scientific reasoning. "Everything in the Universe is governed by laws. The Universe is one vast chemical laboratory, in constant operation, by her internal forces," Rose argued. "Had man been a patient and impartial inquirer, and not . . . attributed everything he could not understand to supernatural causes . . . but [instead] observed the operations of Nature, he would undoubtedly have known more, been wiser, and happier." She gave an example of this scientific knowledge, pointing to advances in geology that contradicted the biblical creation story: "Revelation tells us that the world was created in six days. Here Geology steps in and says that it requires thousands of ages to form the various strata of the earth."[34]

In the late nineteenth century, a scientific revolution brought about in part by Louis Pasteur's contributions to chemistry and microbiology, and by Charles Darwin's work on evolution, *The Origin of Species* (1859), would soon transform America and the rest of the world. Darwin's theories on natural selection and evolution would gain wide acceptance in the United States during Rose's lifetime, while at the same time stirring up controversy.[35]

Rose faced hostility from many Christians, who accused "infidels" of being immoral, and from nativists who were prejudiced against immigrants.

She mentioned to Susan B. Anthony during their trip to the South that she felt betrayed by some colleagues in the reform movement who had expressed xenophobic views.[36] Rose faced another challenge that was even more pernicious—rising anti-Semitism, beginning in the Civil War era. In her speech at the Seventh National Woman's Rights Convention, she spoke of the heroism of "the woman who stands up for the right . . . who face[s] the fire of an unjust and prejudiced public opinion, [who] brave[s] not only the enemy abroad, but often that severest of all enemies, your own friends at home. [This] requires a heroism that the world has never yet recognized . . . "[37] Speaking here indirectly about herself, she was implying that as a Jew and an atheist she was not accepted by many in the reform movement.

Wendell Phillips, a prominent abolitionist, advocate for women's rights and for Native American rights, was one of the reformers who harbored anti-Semitic feelings. He said at the Seventh National Woman's Rights Convention: "Woman has gained right after right . . . with us . . . She stands almost side by side with man in her civil rights. The Saxon race has led the van. I trample underfoot contemptuously the Jewish—yes, the Jewish—ridicule which laughs at such a Convention as this; for we are the Saxon blood."[38] Phillips showed support for white, Anglo-Saxon, Protestant women but spoke disparagingly of Jews and presumably of other minority women.

At the 1860 convention, Phillips made a distinction between the teachings of Jesus, representing "good" Christianity, and that of St. Paul, who was in his view tainted by Jewish practices: "St. Paul . . . is the noblest figure in all history, except that of Christ . . . but he was a Jew and not a Christian; he lived under Jewish civilization and not ours, and was speaking by his own light, and not by inspiration of God."[39] Phillips' words undoubtedly offended Rose. The two activists stood side by side at women's rights conventions, advocating universal human rights. Phillips' anti-Jewish bias completely undercut the progressive spirit of his speeches. While Rose often attacked religion and the church, she was attacking principles and not specific people or religious communities.

A writer later reflecting on the women's rights movement would use anti-Semitic language to describe Paulina Wright Davis and Ernestine Rose as "two women of that extreme type of so-called reformers now known as socialists or anarchists . . . who would overturn the state altogether and with it all the institutions of Christian civilization."[40]

How can we make sense of the prolonged heated written debate between two friends who were atheists and freethinkers—Horace Seaver, editor of the radical freethought newspaper, the *Boston Investigator*—and Ernestine Rose? Here were two people who presumably knew each other very well, who were both committed to rational thought and to "mental freedom." The motto of the *Boston Investigator* was: "Devoted to the development and promotion of universal mental and religious liberty." Over the course of more than five months, from October 1863 to April 1864, Seaver made anti-Semitic comments about Jewish people, both ancient Israelites and modern Jews, to which Rose responded, staunchly defending the Jews. Seaver, as editor, controlled the debate by dividing Rose's letters in half, spreading each letter over two weeks, and following each of her letters with his "Remarks," thereby ensuring that he would always have the last word.

Set in the historic context of the Civil War years, Seaver's comments reflect the widespread, rising anti-Semitism in America, which would continue into the twentieth century and beyond. This was the era in which General Ulysses Grant issued his infamous Order No. 11, which charged the Jews, "as a class," with "violating every regulation of trade" established by authorities. Jews were given twenty-four hours to leave the war zone. Although Grant's order was later rescinded and the charges found to be exaggerated or false, this case showed the pervasive anti-Semitic attitude of this period.[41]

Seaver's editorial of October 28, 1863 triggered a "debate on the Jews," by his comments:

> The ancient Jews were said to be the chosen people of God . . . and we should naturally expect them to be the best people who have ever lived . . . ; instead of which, they were about the worst people of whom we have any account . . . Modern Jews appear much better in history than their ancient brethren. Perhaps this was owing to their loss of power and their being scattered among other nations, which has rendered them comparatively harmless. It was a lucky thing for their immediate neighbors that the Jews were scattered, for they were a troublesome people to live in proximity with . . . The Jews still cling with wonderful tenacity to the old religious superstition of Moses with all its absurd rites and ceremonies.

Rose responded by reminding Seaver that in every debate, "principles and not persons were to be discussed . . . The *Investigator*, with its noble motto, its advocacy of equal justice to all irrespective of sect, has always endeavored to keep that distinction in view." Believing she had set the ground rules for their discussion, she continued: "As the (modern) Jews are really very little known . . . it may be well to give a cursory glance not only at their religion, but at them as a people." She then proceeded to describe Judaism: "[It] is a belief in one God, Deism—true Unitarianism, in which Thomas Paine, Thomas Jefferson [and] Voltaire . . . believed." As for modern Jews, Rose said that while they have distinguishing traditions and ceremonies, "[they] are in general as liberal as Universalists . . . In spite of the barbarous treatment and deadly persecution they suffered, they have lived . . . and Europe has been none the worse on their account." Rose was separating myths about Jews from the reality of modern Jewish life, in an attempt to engage Seaver in a rational, fact-based discussion. She was also showing that she had knowledge of modern Jewish practices, despite her break with Judaism.

Rose's attempts at rational discussion with Seaver did not succeed. Each successive exchange of letters became more heated and divisive. Seaver ignored the ground rules proposed by Rose and continually resorted to anti-Semitic stereotypes: "The ancient Jews, . . . a rude and barbarous people, will always have a rude and barbarous God . . . The Universalists, . . . being a much better people . . . have a much better God and more benevolent religion." Rose responded again by demonstrating how negative myths about Jews were false: "[Jews] progressed in their traditions and made great innovations . . . " She concluded her letter with a second reminder to Seaver: " . . . Let the subject be impartially investigated."

Seaver defended his arguments: "Of course, we were speaking of them as a religious sect. We have nothing against a Jew personally and never persecuted one in any way . . . " He persisted, however, in resorting to Jewish stereotypes—their obsession with money, their dealing in "old clothes"—and he mocked their European accent ("fifteen per shent"), showing that he was unable to distinguish between racist stereotypes and reality. "Of all the people we ever read of," Seaver continued, "we do not know of any so completely vile, worthless, miserable, contemptible and abominable as the ancient Jews." Rose rebuked him once more for his attacks, complaining that "[Jews are] an inoffensive sect who suffer quite enough from Christian prejudice without the help of Infidels." She was undoubtedly thinking here about her own family's experience of oppression in Poland.

Rose's frustration with Seaver grew with each exchange of letters, as he continued to make unfounded accusations against Jews, both ancient and modern, and as he mocked her: "Perhaps she [Rose] may be thinking of turning Jew." Her anger burst forth: "How do you know that the modern Jews are what you describe them to be? . . . You make unwarrantable assertions which convict you out of your own mouth of as much folly and bigotry . . . Pray keep Judaism and the Jew distinct!" She reminded him, in case he had forgotten, that she herself was Jewish: "Is it possible that you 'know of no other Jew who has left the barbarism of Moses for the philosophy of the *Investigator*?' Try, you may find one besides 'the Rose that all are praising' [one of Seaver's phrases describing her in the *Investigator*]."[42]

How do we interpret Rose's forceful defense of the Jews and her denunciation of Seaver's attacks? While she had given up all formal ties to Judaism, she demonstrated that she remained strongly committed to Jewish peoplehood and values from her upbringing as a member of this religious sect. As shown earlier, it is likely that Rose's Jewish identity and her family history, growing up under oppression in Poland, are what had first drawn her to pursue justice and equal rights. America, with its protection of minority rights and its freedom, offered the promise of a more just society. How infuriating it must have been for her, then, to hear the editor of a freethought newspaper uttering racist remarks and refusing to adhere to the principles of rational thought and tolerance that his newspaper ostensibly espoused!

Rose's anger was provoked in large part by her moral stand as a spokesperson for human rights. Just as she passionately spoke out against slavery and racial inequality in America, so did she strongly defend the Jews against anti-Semitism and stereotyping throughout much of her adult life. A newspaper editor of the *Jewish Record*, who had been following the controversy, commented that although Ernestine Rose had abandoned her religion, she still possessed "some of the old leaven of the Jewish spirit . . . "[43] Seaver and Rose remained entrenched in their respective positions at the end of the debate but would later reconcile and resume their friendship.

Rose exerted an influence as a powerful orator and freethinker on one of the best known American poets, Walt Whitman. Whitman and Rose became acquainted during the 1850's. The two New Yorkers, both freethinkers and strong supporters of women's rights, shared an admiration for Thomas Paine and Frances Wright. Whitman and Rose put their faith in the promise of American democracy to bring about broad-based reform and to bring into mainstream society those persons—women, immigrants, minorities—that society had excluded. Whitman recalled the effect that Rose's words had on him, as he remarked to his friend Horace Traubel:

> I remember Mrs. Ernestine L. Rose—the big, noble woman!—when speaking of the [French] Revolution . . . her eyes would flash—and she would exclaim—'What!—to be trod down and not turn! Do you take the people to be of wood or of stone!' Oh! her eye, her cheek, her way, her half-rising from the chair—it was all fine. And the words are as strong, I put them there in my notebook—have kept them all these years.[44]

Whitman borrowed some of Rose's words for his poem, "France, The 18th Year of These States," in *Leaves of Grass*. He was commemorating the French Revolution and France's march towards freedom:

> Could I wish humanity different?
> Could I wish the people made of wood and stone? Or that there be no justice in destiny or time?[45]

His 1860 poem, "Thought," reflected his views on freethought and democracy, with words that remind us of Rose's oratory:

> . . . Of the mumbling and screaming priest (soon, soon deserted)

... Of the rising forever taller and stronger and broader of the institutions of men and women, and of Self-Esteem and Personality;
... Of the true New World—of the Democracies resplendent
en-masse ...[46]

Whitman, like Rose, hoped to see all Americans fully exercising their
inherent, natural rights. He expressed his dream of seeing religious, political and military institutions taking their cue from the democratic will of the
people, rather than exerting their authority over the nation.

Rose noted with satisfaction, writing to the *Boston Investigator* in 1860,
that attitudes regarding "mental freedom" were evolving in a positive way.
She had been invited to give a lecture on education in Flushing, Queens, but
a minister had attempted to dissuade his congregation from attending it, saying, "I would never allow a daughter of mine to listen to such a woman!" She
was pleasantly surprised to see both women and men in attendance to hear
her speak on education and religion. Rose commented on the progress she
had observed:

In spite of the constant effort of Puritanism to keep the human mind in check,
and prevent mental freedom, 'the world moves,' slowly it is true, but surely;
and though ... the purifying process of agitation had never dispersed the fog of
superstition from [some] minds, yet it requires but very little to raise a whole-
some breeze to agitate the stagnant elements; and the atmosphere once set in
motion, who can impede its progress of purifying the mental as well as the
physical miasmas?[47]

Rose anticipated the growing prestige of science, which would lead a majority of people to concur with rationalist theories, including evolution, rather
than to accept fundamentalist interpretations of scripture.[48] Liberal American
religious congregations would reflect the growing influence of rationalist
thought by finding areas where reason and faith were mutually compatible.
Many churches and synagogues would become more democratic, egalitarian
and inclusive by the twentieth century.[49]

Rose's contributions to religious and intellectual freedom received recognition during her lifetime. A weekly newspaper, *The Hebrew Leader*, referred
to Rose as "the earliest and noblest among the workers in the cause of human
enfranchisement," and "an ardent adherent of moral Judaism."[50] Several
Unitarian ministers, including Moncure D. Conway, Thomas Wentworth
Higginson and Edward F. Strickland, expressed their admiration for her work.
Reverend Strickland wrote to her in Brighton, England to request a copy of
her photograph. Rose thanked him for his "interest in reform movements."[51]

Had Rose lived in the twenty-first century, she would have probably con-
curred with a journalist on National Public Radio who spoke about America's

adherence to a nonsectarian "civil religion," based on a collection of beliefs, symbols, and rituals inspired by its founding documents. The commentator, Tom Gjelten, argued: "The strength and binding power of America's civil religion is clearly being put to a test." "Our 'Scriptures,'" said Gjelten, "need to be constantly updated to be more inclusive of the country's diverse ethnic, racial and religious communities."[52] Rose would have shared Gjelten's view that America must continue its arduous struggle to be more progressive and inclusive, in order to live up to its secular founding principles.

NOTES

1. Bonnie S. Anderson, *The Rabbi's Atheist Daughter: Ernestine Rose, International Feminist Pioneer* (New York: Oxford University Press, 2017), 51.

2. Anderson, 101; George Jacob Holyoake (1817–1906) would give the eulogy at Ernestine Rose's funeral. See "Eulogy for Ernestine L. Rose" in Paula Doress-Worters, ed., *Mistress of Herself: Speeches and Letters of Ernestine L. Rose, Early Women's Rights Leader* (New York: The Feminist Press, 2008), 357–358.

3. David L. Holmes,"The Founding Fathers, Deism and Christianity," Encyclopedia Britannica, https://www.britannica.com/topic/The-Founding-Fathers-Deism-and-Christianity-1272214.

4. Thomas Jefferson, Letter to the Danbury Baptists, 1802, Library of Congress.

5. Susan Jacoby, *Freethinkers: A History of American Secularism* (New York: Metropolitan Books, 2004), 29.

6. *Papers of George Washington,* Library of Congress, vol. 6: 284–285.

7. Jacoby, 27–32.

8. Morris Schappes, *A Documentary History of the Jews in the United States, 1654–1875* (New York: Schocken, 1971), 235–246.

9. Ernestine L. Rose, "Speech at the Third National Woman's Rights Convention, September 8, 1852," in Doress-Worters, 121.

10. Ginzberg, "The Heathen Wing: Reflections on Secular Jewish Traditions" *Bridges* (Summer 1998): 10–11, JSTOR.

11. See Rose's letters in response to Horace Mann's lectures and her address, *A Defence of Atheism*, discussed later in this chapter.

12. Isaac Deutscher, "The Non-Jewish Jew," *The Non-Jewish Jew and other Essays* (London: Verso, 2017), 26–27.

13. Robert Owen, "The Catechism of the New Moral World," *Bristol Selected Pamphlets* (University of Bristol Library: 1830), https://www.jstor.org/stable/60228964; Paula Doress-Worters, ed., "Madame Rose: A Life of Ernestine L. Rose as told to Jenny P. d'Héricourt," *Journal of Women's History* 15, no. 1 (Spring 2003), ProQuest Ebrary.

14. Carol A. Kolmerten, *The American Life of Ernestine L. Rose* (Syracuse: Syracuse University Press, 1999), 46–47.

15. Gilbert Vale, Editor of the *Beacon,* describes Rose's speech in this newspaper on December 23, 1837, in Kolmerten, 35.

16. Ernestine L. Rose, "Speech at the New England Social Reform Convention, May 30, 1844," in Doress-Worters, 63.

17. Ernestine L. Rose, quoted in Sara A. Underwood, "Ernestine L. Rose," *Heroines of Free Thought* (New York: C. P. Somerby, 1876), 272–273.

18. Ernestine L. Rose, "Speech for Paine Anniversary," *Boston Investigator*, February 18, 1857, 4.

19. Thomas Paine, *The Age of Reason* (1793–1794), quoted in Holmes.

20. Ernestine L. Rose, "Speech at the Thomas Paine Celebration, January 29, 1850," in Doress-Worters, 76–79.

21. Carole Gray, "Nineteenth-Century Women of Freethought," *Free Inquiry* 15, no. 2 (Spring 1995), Gale Document: GALEA16871567.

22. Ernestine L. Rose, *A Defence of Atheism: A Lecture Delivered on April 10, 1861* (Boston: J. P. Mendum, 1881), 18.

23. Bertram W. Korn, "The Rabbis and the Slavery Question," *American Jewry and the Civil War* (New York: Atheneum, 1970), 15–18.

24. Hasia R. Diner, *The Jews of the United States, 1654–2000* (Berkeley: University of California Press, 2004), 156.

25. Korn, 20–22.

26. Morris Schappes, *The Jews in the United States: a Pictorial History, 1654 to the Present* (New York: Citadel Press, 1958), 87.

27. Gray, "Women of Freethought," Gale Document: GALEA16871567.

28. Ernestine L. Rose, "Reviews of Horace Mann's Two Lectures, February–March 1852," in Doress-Worters, ed., *Mistress of Herself*, 108–120.

29. Ernestine L. Rose, "Debate at the Third National Woman's Rights Convention, September 9, 1852," in Doress-Worters, ed., *Mistress of Herself*, 125.

30. Ernestine L. Rose, "Speech at the Hartford Bible Convention, June 4, 1853," in Doress-Worters, ed., *Mistress of Herself*, 142–144.

31. Ernestine L. Rose, "Letter to the Editor: Describing the Hartford Bible Convention, June 14, 1853," in Doress-Worters, ed., *Mistress of Herself*, 145.

32. Wendell Phillips Garrison, Francis Jackson Garrison, *William Lloyd Garrison, the Story of his Life, Told by his Children* (New York: The Century Company, 1885–1889), 385.

33. Ernestine L. Rose, "Speeches at the Seventh National Woman's Rights Convention, November 26, 1856," in Doress-Worters, ed., *Mistress of Herself*, 226–227.

34. Ernestine L. Rose, *A Defence of Atheism,* 7, 15.

35. Jacoby, 125–129.

36. Susan B. Anthony, "Diary of Lecture Tour to the Border South with Ernestine L. Rose," in Doress-Worters, ed., *Mistress of Herself*, 173.

37. Ernestine L. Rose, "Speeches at the Seventh National Woman's Rights Convention, November 26, 1856," quoted in Elizabeth Cady Stanton, Susan B. Anthony, Matilda Joslyn Gage, eds., *History of Woman Suffrage,* vol. 1: 664, Gutenberg E-book.

38. Wendell Phillips is quoted in Stanton, Anthony, Gage, eds., *History of Woman Suffrage,* vol. 1: 637.

39. Phillips is quoted in *History of Woman Suffrage,* vol. 1:705.

40. Caroline F. Corbin, "Woman's Rights in America, 1848–1908" (New York: *New York State Association Opposed to Woman Suffrage*, 1913), 2.

41. A.S. Lindemann, *Esau's Tears: Modern Anti-Semitism and the Rise of the Jews* (New York: Cambridge University Press, 1997), 262, cited in Sandra J. Berkowitz and Amy C. Lewis, "Debating Anti-Semitism: Ernestine Rose vs. Horace Seaver in the *Boston Investigator, 1863–1864,"* *Communication Quarterly* 46, no. 4 (Fall 1998): 457–471.

42. Ernestine L. Rose and Horace Seaver, "Debate on the Jews in the *Boston Investigator*, October 28, 1863 to April 13, 1864," in Doress-Worters, ed., *Mistress of Herself*, 311–333.

43. Yuri Suhl, *Ernestine Rose and the Battle for Human Rights* (New York: Reynal, 1959), 224.

44. Walt Whitman is quoted in Horace Traubel, *With Walt Whitman in Camden*, vol. 6: 322–323 (Carbondale: Southern Illinois University Press, 1982).

45. Walt Whitman, *Variorum,* 2: 241, cited in Sherry Ceniza, *Walt Whitman and 19th Century Women Reformers* (Tuscaloosa: University of Alabama Press, 1998), 140–141.

46. Walt Whitman, *Variorum,* 2:351–352. For more discussion on Whitman's and Rose's views on democracy, see Ceniza, 140–180.

47. Ernestine L. Rose, "The World Moves!" *Boston Investigator*, August 29, 1860, 2.

48. Jacoby, 125–129.

49. See, for example, Mordecai M. Kaplan, *Judaism as a Civilization: Toward a Reconstruction of American Jewish Life* (Philadelphia: Jewish Publication Society, 1981).

50. *The Hebrew Leader*, May 21, 1869, 1.

51. Ernestine L. Rose, "Letter to Reverend Edward F. Strickland," August 30, 1887, in American Jewish Archives, Klau Library, Cincinnati, Ohio.

52. Tom Gjelten, "Can America's 'Civil Religion' Still Unite the Country?" *All Things Considered*, April 12, 2021, NPR.org.

Chapter 7

Late Autumn Harvest

Ernestine Rose was a social reformer whose ideas were often too far ahead of her time to be accepted during her lifetime. Despite her fame, she often referred to herself as a "minority of one."[1] She did live long enough to see some of her "young plants grow strong enough to brave the storm and bear fruit."[2] The Married Women's Property Act of 1860 and Wyoming's adoption of women's suffrage in 1869 were important women's rights achievements credited to her efforts.

Her knowledge of European and American history and her experiences as an immigrant, an "outsider," led her to declare: "Liberty cannot exist without equality of rights—and as long as we have the favored few, must we also have the injured many, and under such a state of things, liberty is only an empty sound."[3] Although America has made much progress since Rose's lifetime, the ideal of an inclusive, democratic, egalitarian society still remains elusive in the first decades of the twenty-first century.

It is not surprising that Ernestine and William Rose chose to move to England in 1869. Rose's growing health issues—she suffered from rheumatism, neuralgia and lung problems—would have made them choose a country like England, known for its health spas. While we have no record of William Rose's thoughts on this, it is possible that he expressed a desire to return to his homeland.

Just seventeen days before their departure, Ernestine Rose applied for and received American citizenship. William Rose had long ago become an American citizen. Rose never wrote about her decision to become an American citizen or about why she had waited so long to apply for citizenship. We can speculate that this choice reflected her strong preference for being a citizen of a democratic republic. She might have delayed her application in the hope of gaining the franchise and being able to exercise her full rights as a citizen. She compounded the mystery of her citizenship by declaring in England two years later: "I am not an American, although I have my residence in the United States," words contradicted by documented proof of her citizenship.[4]

Did the Roses intend to return to America or to settle permanently in England? We cannot be certain but it seems likely that they planned to return to America. Rose would maintain strong ties with Susan B. Anthony and Elizabeth C. Stanton for the rest of her life. Just days before the Roses left for England, Anthony and Stanton had appointed her to the Executive Committee of the National Woman Suffrage Association. The Roses would return for a ten-month stay in New York in 1873–1874. Back in England after this visit, Rose would write to Anthony on July 4, 1876: "Keep a warm place for me with the American people. I hope someday to be there yet." The Roses' financial losses and Ernestine Rose's growing health problems would unfortunately prevent them from coming back again.[5]

Rose's health improved in the short term as she and her husband traveled in France, Switzerland, Germany and England, where they visited health spas. Kate N. Doggett, a Chicago feminist friend of Ernestine Rose, wrote of her:

> [Ernestine Rose's] friends will be glad to know that she is much better than when she left America . . . As I looked into her bright eyes and saw the color deepen in her cheeks as she talked of the good cause she has by no means relinquished on this side of the Atlantic, I could hardly persuade myself that she was an invalid. She has nerve power now to supply a dozen average women, or men either, for that matter.

Recalling that freezing winds had prevented Ernestine and William Rose from crossing the Alps, Doggett concluded, "I think the mistral is the only obstacle by which Ernestine L. Rose was ever vanquished."[6] The Roses wintered in Bath, England, a town known for its hot springs and mineral waters.

Less than a year after the Roses' departure for Europe, the *Boston Investigator* reported a curious omission in *The Revolution*, the same New York newspaper that had published Kate Doggett's glowing account of Ernestine Rose a few months earlier. The paper had omitted Rose's name from a list of major women's rights advocates. The editor of the *Investigator*, shocked, made this observation: " . . . No woman who has been before the public for the last thirty years has labored more perseveringly and effectually in every good cause tending to increase human happiness and improvement [than Rose.]"

The editor suggested a possible reason for this glaring omission: "She has never received anything like a proper appreciation . . . Why is this? We don't know, unless it is because she is a heretic in religion . . . To omit *her* name from the catalogue [of women's rights advocates] is like playing *Hamlet* with the character of Hamlet left out." What made it even harder to accept was that *The Revolution*, a New York newspaper, had apparently forgotten her, since New York City was where the Roses had always lived. He concluded, ruefully: "So goes the world, especially with the unpopular; and this is their reward. 'Out of sight, out of mind.'"[7]

Far from settling down to a quiet retired life in Europe, Rose, now in her sixties, renewed her contacts with reformers, attended conferences and began to give lectures in several European countries on freethought, women's rights, human rights and peace. In Paris, she saw Charles Lemonnier, who, along with Giuseppe Garibaldi and Victor Hugo, had helped to establish the International League of Peace and Freedom. Rose wrote: "I received a pressing invitation from M. Lemonnier to attend the next [Peace] Congress, to be held in Zurich on the 12th of September [1870] . . . The Peace League publishes an interesting paper with the title, 'Les États-Unis d'Europe' (United States of Europe)." Its goal was to achieve peace by establishing a single republican nation in Europe. This early notion of a cooperative organization in Europe was perhaps a forerunner of the European Union.

While in Paris, she also met with a women's rights activist, Léon Richer, "one of the most indefatigable friends of women's rights in France"; and with André Léo (Léodile Champseix), a feminist journalist and novelist. The French women's movement was gaining importance during the Second Empire, despite Napoléon III's authoritarian regime, and it would grow even more during the Third Republic (1870–1940), as journalists and writers widely publicized the need to improve women's condition.[8]

Though forgotten by some in America, Rose was soon taking Europe by storm. The English press began to spotlight her extraordinary oratorical skills. Moncure D. Conway, a friend of the Roses in London, wrote of her: "By a local journal I learned that a startling episode occurred at a public meeting . . . A fine-looking, middle-aged lady arose, ascended the platform, and . . . made a speech on the woman question . . . which fairly revolutionized the meeting . . . "[9]

Here is what had occurred. The Roses were attending a meeting in Bath, England, in the winter of 1870 on the subject of nominating female candidates for the school board. In Great Britain, women spoke far less in public than in the United States in the 1870's. At this meeting, the chairman read aloud a letter from a wealthy philanthropist, Angela Burdett-Coutts, who argued against women participating in politics and holding public office. This roused Ernestine Rose to walk up to the platform and to address the gathering:

I have come to the continent of Europe from beyond, as it is sometimes termed, 'the great pond'—the other side of the Atlantic . . . There, it is almost a settled fact that woman is a human being; that she has a mind, and that mind requires cultivation, that she has wants and needs, which wants and needs require assistance. Hence, we are over there—don't be frightened at the name—a 'Woman's Rights' people; and if ever that should stare you clearly in the face in this country, simply remember that 'woman's rights' simply means 'human rights' and that no woman earnest enough to claim those rights would for one moment have them based on the wrongs of any human being . . . We claim that she shall be able to bring up our children . . . assist our manhood, and aid the great family of man to become healthy, intelligent, and happy members of society.[10]

Rose's speech was greeted with cheers, laughter and great applause. Moved by the power of her words, two women ran as candidates and were later elected to the school board.

The National Reformer, a secularist weekly British newspaper, also took notice of Rose's address in Bath: "*The* speech of the meeting was . . . made by a lady whose name will be familiar to all readers of the *Boston Investigator.* We mean Mrs. Ernestine L. Rose, of New York. The good old lady with her white curls, her erect, healthy-looking body, her clear, distinct voice, her occasional quaint phrases, her stern determination, and her real genius as a speaker, won from those present a far more hearty and lengthened tribute of applause than was accorded to anyone else."[11] The *National Reformer*'s editor, Charles Bradlaugh, would become a close friend and supporter of Ernestine Rose.

Launched on a speaking career in Great Britain, Rose continued to address the public in meetings in London and Edinburgh, Scotland. She spoke on women's rights, Owenism, freethought and human rights. The Roses decided to move to London, where they would live from 1871 to 1873. On the occasion of the centenary of Robert Owen's birth, Rose gave a talk that was received with a "hearty and lengthy tribute of applause."[12] Moncure D. Conway noted: "Mrs. Ernestine L. Rose is something of a lioness in London . . . South Place Chapel was crowded with a thousand people to hear her address upon Robert Owen, and . . . three times applause began and had to be checked."[13] Conway, a Unitarian minister who had long ago rejected the heritage of his slaveholding Virginia family and had moved to London, shared Rose's admiration for Robert Owen and Thomas Paine.[14]

Two days after her address at South Place Chapel, Rose spoke at a large "Festival" to celebrate the centenary birthday of Robert Owen. She was the only female lecturer there. Rose praised Owen for his principles, which she said had contributed to important reforms in society:

He was the man of one idea, and that idea the happiness of the human race . . . He broadcast the notion that the character of man was made *for* him and not *by* him. The effect of a divergence from this view is the present irrational state of society—ignorance, poverty, vice and crime . . . It has been said that he was a fanatic! Whoever did anything good without being a fanatic? . . . What reforms there have been for the last twenty years have been the product of the principles promulgated by Robert Owen. Education, industry, economy, the various societies for mutual assistance, and particularly, I remark, the temperance reform, the prison reformation; and I have no doubt that he would have advocated the Women's Rights Bill, had he lived . . . [Human beings] are the creatures of the influences by which they are surrounded. The nature of man is good.[15]

While the experimental socialist community in Skaneateles, New York, did not endure for many years, some of Owen's principles, promoted by Rose and other activists, did take hold in America. Considering men and women mainly as products of their social environment, rather than as being inherently good or evil, reformers worked to establish free public education, improved working conditions in industry, and prison reforms that would rehabilitate criminals. The establishment of labor unions and addiction treatment would also follow Owenite principles.

Rose spoke in Edinburgh in February 1873 in favor of a bill by Liberal M. P. Jacob Bright to give women the franchise. She was *the* speaker of the evening in the crowded hall, according to the Edinburgh *Daily Review*. Rose immediately charmed the crowd as she began to speak:

Two years ago some opposition was heard in the House of Commons against Mr. Jacob Bright's bill [in favor of woman suffrage] . . . But what were the arguments against it? . . . One argument against the bill was that woman was not logical—Now, really, I am not going to stand here to prove that I am logical; I only meant to say that that was an illogical argument—for the franchise was never given for logic. Had it been based upon logic, I doubt whether that member of Parliament would ever have been in his place . . . He was not a member of Parliament because he was logical; therefore he had a perfect right to be as illogical as he pleased . . . (Laughter and applause).[16]

Having won over her audience by her wit, Rose then spoke seriously and passionately about the benefits of woman suffrage for society:

It was as self-evident as that two and two make four that human beings under the same conditions ought to have the same general rights; and where were the conditions that were so different in this case? Humanity recognizes no sex, morality recognizes no sex—pleasure and pain, virtue and vice, life and death recognize no sex . . . What elevated man will not degrade woman (Applause). If woman had the franchise, it would elevate her in the public mind and . . . elevate her in her own estimation . . . She would take a higher aim and higher object in life . . . endeavoring to make the world happier and better from having lived in it. . . .

It was a puerile and frivolous argument that woman, if she got the franchise, would cease to be womanly . . . She might become stronger in mind, more faithful to convictions; she might become more intellectual; she might take a greater and wider view of the duties and responsibilities of life . . . Would that change her nature? . . . No! Believe, trust in the right, do rightly, do justly, and leave all the consequences to themselves (Loud applause).[17]

Rose's Edinburgh speech echoed the principle, expressed both by Owen and by the authors of the Declaration of Independence, that all human beings had natural rights. According to Rose, everyone had the same potential for self-awareness and self-development, but social conditions often limited a person's capacity to fulfill his potential. It was therefore imperative to reform society in order to restore these rights. Rose completely rejected the widespread nineteenth-century belief that women were inherently different from men and should therefore be limited to the domestic sphere.

At the conclusion of the Edinburgh meeting, attendees passed a resolution supporting Jacob Bright's bill. Bright succeeded in getting the bill for women's local suffrage passed in Parliament; in addition, he supported married women's property rights and women's national suffrage.[18] A Chicago columnist would later write that among the principal events affecting the political and civil life of British women in the 1870's were the School Board Act, the election of the first women to the school board and the Married Women's Property Amendment Act, all passed in 1870. Rose had played a role, directly or indirectly, in all of these acts. Her speech in Bath had persuaded women to run for election to the school board for the first time. In addition, Rose's contributions to the Married Women's Property Act of 1860 in America may have served as a model for the British law.[19]

In August 1873, the Roses sailed back to New York City after having lived in Europe for four years. They arrived in a city that had undergone notable changes. With a dramatic increase in its population in the 1870's, the city faced a housing crisis: new building construction lagged behind, while millions of immigrants continued to pour into the city. This led to crowded tenement buildings in the Lower East Side, in which five or six families shared a single floor. Apartment rooms were often narrow and dilapidated, with little air or sunlight. Many buildings still had no indoor plumbing. More than half of Manhattan's tenements were "in a condition detrimental to the health and dangerous to the lives of the occupants."[20]

In an effort to remedy this, Albany enlarged its Department of Buildings and established the nation's first building codes to regulate and improve sanitary conditions. Urban planners and developers began to make extensive improvements in the city, attempting to emulate what the Baron Haussmann had accomplished in Paris. Landscape architects Frederick L. Olmsted and his partner Calvert Vaux created Central Park, a pastoral refuge from noise and pollution for New Yorkers. It would become a model for future urban planners.[21]

As social reformers, the Roses would have been pleased at the growing bargaining power of New York labor unions, which fought for eight-hour workdays, improved working conditions and increased wages. Susan B. Anthony and Elizabeth C. Stanton helped to organize the Workingwomen's Association to lobby on behalf of women, who worked primarily as seamstresses and typographers. Women represented a growing percentage of the labor force. The Workingwomen's Association, though short-lived because of internal conflicts between middle-class and working-class unionists, was nevertheless an important development in labor rights.[22]

Rose fell seriously ill in November 1873 with an unnamed malady and was unable to leave her room for weeks. She slowly recovered and was only able to attend one convention—the Sixth Annual Convention of the National Woman Suffrage Association in New York on May 14–15, 1874.[23] Had she attended the National Woman Suffrage Convention held the previous spring, celebrating the twenty-fifth anniversary of the Seneca Falls Convention, Rose would have been pleased to hear that while the 1848 convention had hardly received any press coverage, recent women's rights conventions had gotten international coverage. In the United States, "woman suffrage was the chief political question of the hour."[24]

In Rose's address at the National Woman Suffrage Convention, she argued that "the wonder was not that they had not accomplished more, but that they had accomplished so much." With her internationalist perspective, she commented on conditions in Europe:

> There were distinctions and classes [in Europe], and it was very difficult to make European monarchs recognize the fact that they were no better than the people for whose purposes they are instituted, and it was equally difficult to inspire into men's minds the idea that women were other than their helpmates, and were not created for the same glorious destiny. They might make whatever laws they pleased, but let them make them alike for men and women. What right had man to make laws for her; the laws were binding on her as on man, and all she asked was participation in their formation.

She noted progress in Great Britain: "In England, nearly two hundred members of the House of Commons were in favor of woman suffrage, and there was no doubt it would come into operation there before long." In fact, neither British women nor American women would win the franchise until the twentieth century. After telling the convention that "ill health would prevent her from ever again appearing in public," Rose sat down and was "roundly applauded."[25] This was Rose's last public address in the United States. She and her husband would sail back to England in June.

Before returning to England, the Roses donated four oil paintings, depicting Thomas Paine, Robert Owen, William Rose and Ernestine Rose, to hang in the new Paine Memorial Hall in Boston, an imposing edifice that would serve as the *Boston Investigator*'s headquarters. The building's cornerstone was laid on July 4, 1874, over a box containing photographs, including one of Ernestine Rose, to "inform the Liberals of 1974 or 2000 that we met . . . to honor Thomas Paine." A *New York Times* columnist noted that about 700 people attended the building's dedication ceremony on January 29, 1875, in which they paid tribute to Thomas Paine with speeches "representing all shades of radical belief," with hymns, orchestral music and finally with a celebratory grand ball.[26]

Rose was unable to attend this event but she wrote from England:

> I would like to . . . write a good speech for your glorious occasion, but, alas! I am too ill to do even that, and so I have to console myself with the fact that we will be represented by our four pictures on the walls of your Temple of freethought and free speech . . . But as pictures cannot speak, I will add a few words. Please say to the friends assembled that from across the ocean whose waves roll between us, I welcome them in the name of Universal Mental Freedom. I welcome them in the name of Human Rights, without any distinction of sex, country or color. I welcome them in the name of 'Truth without mystery, mixture of error, or the fear of man.'[27]

She would donate money for many years to fund this building. The *Boston Investigator* rented out Paine Hall for lectures and at one lecture in 1876, Susan B. Anthony remarked, referring to Rose's portrait on the wall, "I am always glad to be in the same vicinity with a picture of that noble worker for the cause of woman's freedom."[28]

The Roses moved to Brighton, England, a city known for its mineral baths and spas, where they hoped to restore Ernestine Rose's health. Their rationale for moving back to England was most likely a practical one—it was more affordable and comfortable for them to live there than in New York. Rose had written a few years earlier about life in England: "When you hire an apartment (large or small), the people of the house engage to keep house for you without any extra charges. We have two large rooms, well-furnished . . . with fire and gas, and all kinds of services . . . Our expenses for living are a little more than $11 [per week]. In New York, to live the same way would cost us from $30 to $40." Since they were getting on in years and having more health issues, they would have found housework increasingly difficult. In addition, they were having financial problems after the Great Chicago Fire of October

1871 and the Boston Fire of November 1872 had destroyed property in which they had investments. Rose would later write to the *Boston Investigator*: " . . . As you know, the Chicago and Boston fires have crippled our means."[29]

Rose sent her observations about the seaside town of Brighton to the *Boston Investigator*: "It is a pleasant town . . . with a high cliff, over three miles long, facing the sea, and graced on the opposite side by fine buildings and stores . . . Brighton is considered a very healthy place . . . but, take it all in all, Brighton, like all other English towns, is very dull, very religious, very anti-progressive . . . "

She then related several anecdotes about her encounters with ministers who were attending a meeting in Brighton. One minister encouraged her to go to a lecture, "Skepticism and Skeptics," even though she didn't have a ticket, by saying that she could make up an excuse to tell the doorkeeper. "Thanks," Rose replied. "But would that not be telling an untruth? And would that be right?" The minister had no response to that.

She attended an "Anti-Woman's Rights" lecture given by a different minister who said: "Woman is Queen *in her husband's house.*" Rose commented, wryly: "Queen over the crockery, jewelry, china, etc." She summed up his address this way: "The whole discourse was made up of Bible quotations, misrepresentations, downright falsehoods, insults and flattery." Just as she had earlier responded to a speaker in Bath, Rose was roused to go up on the platform and address the audience: "I plead guilty to being a Woman's Rights woman," she began. She addressed the crowd for fifteen minutes and later commented: "To my surprise I was well received . . . "[30]

Rose would continue to suffer from health problems during the coming years. She wrote to Susan B. Anthony in January 1877 about her health, in response to Anthony's request for information about herself for the book, *History of Woman Suffrage*:

> Believe me, it would give me great pleasure to comply with your request, to tell you all about myself and my past labors; but I suffer so much from neuralgia in my head and general debility, that I could not undertake the task, especially as I have nothing to refer to. I have never spoken from notes; and as I did not intend to publish anything about myself . . . and did not expect that a Susan B. Anthony would wish to do it for me, I made no memorandum of places, dates, or names.[31]

Why would Ernestine Rose deny her close friend Susan B. Anthony information that might contribute to making herself and their cause better known and appreciated throughout the United States? Rose was no doubt being truthful when she said that she did not usually write down her ideas, preferring instead to use the power of the spoken word as a tool of persuasion. While she was a virtuoso with words and would speak extemporaneously, she was not a prolific writer and had in fact published very little, other than two short books, *An Address on Woman's Rights* (Boston: J. P. Mendum, 1851) and *A Defence of Atheism* (Boston: J. P. Mendum, 1881).

There may have been another reason for her reluctance to write about herself. In 1856 she had written to the *Boston Investigator* that she would be taking a furlough "after twenty years as a volunteer soldier in the cause of Truth."[32] The key word in her description of herself is "soldier." Rose appeared to identify completely with the many causes she championed, much as a soldier identifies with his nation's principles and ideals. She considered herself primarily as an activist. Years later, she would say to a friend, "I have destroyed nearly all the newspaper reports lately [about herself], thinking no one would care to see them."[33] Rose's behavior—the fact that she never accepted a speaker's fee and rarely shared personal information—suggests that she was an altruistic person who was reticent to talk about her private life.

Rose's recovery in 1878 made it possible for her to participate in several conferences. In June 1878, she spoke at length over two days at the "London Conference of Liberal Thinkers, for the Discussion of Matters Pertaining to the Religious Needs of our Time." Her friend Moncure D. Conway had organized the meeting and had invited clergymen of many faiths, as well as freethinkers from England and abroad. On the first day, Ernestine Rose spoke about freethought:

> I profess no religion; and I long ago discarded even the name. What is religion? That term is indefinite and indefinable . . . I am a freethinker to the very fullest extent. I have never yet heard a definition of God that comes up to my conscientious conviction. We can have no progress without liberty of thought, and liberty of thought is not enough . . . We want liberty not only to think but a liberty to express our thoughts. That is a part of progress, irrespective of opinions.[34]

Rose's strong conviction that without liberty of thought, there could be no progress, and that freedom to express one's thoughts was essential to a democracy, had its roots in her personal experiences. In both Europe and America, she had witnessed discrimination, authoritarianism, and persecution. Several of her friends in the freethought community had served time in prison for the crime of blasphemy, including George Holyoake, a British newspaper editor, and Abner Kneeland, the American editor of the *Boston Investigator*.

As she continued speaking, Rose showed her strong anticlericalism: "The Reverend Mr. Voysey and the Reverend Mr. Anybody Else, unless they are too fixed in their bigotry or too much impeded in their religious views, as well as the more rational and liberal Christians, could all unite—all have a perfect right to express their views."[35] Rose's harsh attack on the clergy convinced one attendee to walk out—Reverend Charles Voysey did not return to the conference again. According to Conway's biographer, Rose's speech had convinced Voysey that he could not support freethought and that there could be no alliance between theists and atheists.[36]

Rose made a reference in her address to a *cause célèbre* in England—the trial and conviction of Annie Besant and Charles Bradlaugh, co-editors of the weekly *National Reformer*, for publishing a book on birth control. After their conviction for the offense of "obscenity," a judge overturned the verdict because of a technicality. Annie Besant, a British social reformer, was the first woman to publicly advocate contraceptives. She wrote: "It is clearly useless to preach the limitation of the family and to conceal the means whereby such limitation may be effected." The scandal cost Besant custody of her children in a later divorce settlement, after her husband had persuaded the judge that she was unfit as a mother because of her antireligious views.[37] In the United States, the Comstock Lawof 1873 similarly made it illegal to distribute or publish "obscene" or "immoral" writings, including references to contraception or abortion.

Rose argued forcefully at the Conference of Liberal Thinkers for complete freedom of expression:

> To improve the world, [we must] obtain rational and consistent laws, laws that will not deprive a mother of her child (loud and continued applause)—as has been done to Mrs. Besant, simply because she thinks differently from the judge; laws that will not incarcerate an innocent, respectable man, simply because he sold something he conscientiously thought would benefit society.[38]

In her concluding remarks at the conference, Rose spoke of being in a "minority of one": "I would much rather be in a minority, even of one, for the right, than in a large majority for wrong and oppression. Forty-five years ago it was infinitely more difficult to speak on religion unless you agreed with it. Now it is not so . . . " She was likely referring to blasphemy laws which had criminalized public criticism of religion. Kneeland was the last American to be jailed for this "offense" but some states would continue to have these laws on the books, even in the twenty-first century.[39]

Rose ended her address by summing up her secular humanist philosophy:

> I call all religions superstitions. I cannot vote for what appears to me the great curse of the human mind, the great stumbling block in the way of human progress . . . My pocket is so full of humanity alone, that I have no pocket for anything else. I go for man . . . all the emotion we can possibly possess, all the feelings which human nature is capable of, all belongs to man. If there be one God or ten thousand gods, they do not need it, but man does and woman does . . . Our life is short, and we cannot spare an hour from the human race,

even for all the gods in creation . . . I can say—I wanted to say, 'God speed.' . . . Go on, friends, do all you can, remembering that it is a positive theft from the human race to trouble yourselves about beings, whoever they are, above and beyond man, for they do not need us. I am grateful to the meeting for having listened to such a heretic as I am who cannot recognize anything here beyond the humanity to which we belong.[40]

A reporter for the British *Unitarian Herald* wrote about Rose's speech: "It was the most extraordinary speech I ever heard from a woman; and coming as it did from a lady of advanced years, and spoken as it was with a really deep earnestness, it could not but touch all who listened sympathetically."[41]

Rose anticipated societal changes that would occur in Europe and America. There would be a gradual shift in public discourse on religion in the late nineteenth-century, as most liberal believers accepted scientific reasoning over fundamentalist interpretations of the Bible, while reserving matters of faith to churches, synagogues, mosques and private conscience.[42] Rose, throughout her career, was critical of the ways that some clergymen had misused their authority to defend slavery and to justify denying rights to women, Blacks and other minorities. Rose saw religion as a stumbling block to progress. The First Amendment guaranteed the freedom to express oneself. Yet there were blasphemy and obscenity laws, supported by some conservative judges and clergymen, which took away this right by criminalizing atheism and making it illegal to disseminate information about contraceptives.

She would continue to speak at conferences on women's rights, freethought, human rights and peace until her late sixties, when illness would incapacitate her. Rose attended five peace conferences in Europe. Along with Julia Ward Howe—an abolitionist, women's rights activist, poet and author of "The Battle Hymn of the Republic"—she represented the United States at the International Congress of the Friends of Peace, held in Paris in October 1878. Now somewhat frail at sixty-eight, Rose apologized for her poor French and for not being "strong enough to speak for long."

Despite Rose's physical frailty, the French audience greeted her words with frequent applause and expressions of approbation: "I want to say that women should be represented in these universal peace societies," she began, "because women have as much interest in peace as men do. War is as terrible and even more terrible on women, because if it is unfortunate to lose one's life, it is even more unfortunate to lose those who are dear to us (Applause)."

She then made a personal reference to her experience growing up in Poland: "I have always been against war because, since my youth, I have known what war does: it destroys everything, not only life, but commerce, the sciences, the arts, and what is even worse—morality, virtue (Shouts of approbation). War is the crime of crimes . . . (Shouts of approval)." Rose reminded her audience that she had spoken at several peace conferences in America, Switzerland and London. "In all nations, I am interested in subjects that touch on the reform and elevation of man (Shouts of approbation)." She concluded:

> We can't have peace, because we don't yet completely possess freedom. To obtain peace, you must have freedom, justice, freedom of thought, which is worthless without freedom to express one's opinions (Shouts of approbation). . . . Justice for man, justice for woman, for every human soul. Without freedom, one can't have peace, because you can't remain quiet under the yoke of oppression. Let us then do everything in our power for freedom and against war, and may everywhere men and women be united in this goal![43]

After lengthy applause, other speakers spoke in support of her ideas. A group then proposed a resolution which was unanimously approved: that every peace society would include a "Women's Committee."

Rose's words echoed those she had spoken decades earlier as a young immigrant from Poland, a country "under the yoke of oppression." She had argued that America's vigilance and intervention in international affairs could help to avert wars. Peace without freedom and human rights was a meaningless word. Her remarks at the Paris peace conference were Rose's last public speech.

The last decades of the nineteenth century would see many international women's rights conventions, bringing to fruition Rose's goal of creating a cosmopolitan women's movement. One such organization was the *Association Internationale des Femmes*, created by the Swiss women's rights and peace activist, Marie Goegg. Goegg credited American feminists with inspiring her organization, saying: "The germ deposited in America in 1848, although its growth was difficult, finally took root in Europe."[44] The Women's International League for Peace and Freedom, founded by the American settlement worker Jane Addams in 1915, would continue the work begun by Rose, Anthony and Stanton.[45]

Rose's friends would comfort and support her during the greatest tragedy of her life: the sudden death of William Rose from a heart attack on January 25, 1882. He had collapsed on a street in London, and although bystanders had rushed him to a hospital, he died before reaching it. Charles Bradlaugh wrote of Ernestine Rose: " . . . I found the good old lady very brave but very heartbroken at the loss of her faithful partner."[46]

Josiah Mendum wrote in his obituary of William Rose in the *Boston Investigator*:

> Mr. Rose was a very worthy man in all the relations of life. Pleasant in his manners, prompt in all his duties, and remarkably kind and benevolent in his disposition, he was greatly esteemed by all who enjoyed the pleasure of his

acquaintance. He was a genuine and an intelligent Liberal, made so by reading and reflection, and, although quiet and unassuming, yet his upright example and kind deeds spoke louder than words of the purity and goodness of his mind and heart.[47]

Ernestine Rose's life would not be the same as she faced a future without her beloved husband and life partner.

NOTES

1. Ernestine L. Rose, *The Liberator,* May 29, 1862, 3, quoted in Bonnie S. Anderson, *The Rabbi's Atheist Daughter: Ernestine Rose, International Feminist Pioneer* (Oxford: Oxford University Press, 2017), 123.

2. Rose was describing metaphorically reformers' setbacks and achievements in "Authoresses to the Rescue," *The Revolution,* December 28, 1868, 43.

3. Ernestine L. Rose, "Speech at the Thomas Paine Celebration, January 29, 1849," in Paula Doress-Worters, ed., *Mistress of Herself: Speeches and Letters of Ernestine L. Rose, Early Women's Rights Leader* (New York: The Feminist Press, 2008), 73.

4. Ernestine L. Rose, quoted in *Report of the Proceedings of the Festival in Commemoration of the Centenary Birthday Celebration of Robert Owen, held in London, May 16, 1871,* https://openlibrary.org, 20–21; A copy of Rose's citizenship document is found in the Yuri Suhl Papers, Box 15, Howard Gotlieb Archives, Boston University.

5. Anderson,140. The Roses' financial losses were caused in part by fires in Chicago and Boston that destroyed property they had invested in; Ernestine L. Rose, "Letter to Susan B. Anthony," July 4, 1876, in Doress-Worters, 346.

6. Kate N. Doggett, "Letter from Lisbon," *The Revolution,* March 3, 1870, 135.

7. "Mrs. Ernestine L. Rose," *Boston Investigator,* July 20, 1870, 6.

8. Ernestine L. Rose, "Letter," *Boston Investigator,* July 20, 1870; Theodore Stanton, "Continental Europe," in Elizabeth Cady Stanton, Susan B. Anthony, Matilda Joslyn Gage, eds., *History of Woman Suffrage,* vol. 3: 896–897, Gutenberg E-book.

9. Moncure D. Conway is quoted in Sara A. Underwood, "Ernestine L. Rose," *Heroines of Free Thought* (New York: C. P. Somerby, 1876), 275–276.

10. Ernestine L. Rose, "Letter," *Boston Investigator,* March 1, 1871, 347.

11. The *National Reformer* article is cited in Underwood, 276.

12. "Ernestine L. Rose," *Boston Investigator,* May 24, 1871, 5.

13. "Mrs. Ernestine L. Rose in London," *Boston Investigator,* July 5, 1871, 6.

14. Anderson, 145.

15. Ernestine L. Rose, *Centenary Birthday Celebration of Robert Owen,* 20–21.

16. "A Speech by Mrs. Ernestine L. Rose on Woman's Suffrage," *Boston Investigator,* February 26, 1873, 3. I have changed the third-person form of address to the first-person form ("I"), which Rose would have used.

17. Rose, "Woman's Suffrage," 3.

18. Rose, "Woman's Suffrage," 3; Anderson, 144.

19. Mrs. Elizabeth Boynton Harbert, "Woman's Kingdom," *Daily Inter Ocean,* August 10, 1878, 11.

20. Edwin G. Burrows and Mike Wallace, *Gotham: A History of New York City to 1898* (New York: Oxford University Press, 1999), 921.

21. Burrows and Wallace, 921–923.

22. Burrows and Wallace, 988–991.

23. Anderson, 152–153.

24. Stanton, Anthony, and Gage, eds., *History of Woman Suffrage,* vol. 2: 585, Gutenberg E-book.

25. "Women Who Want to Vote," *New York Times,* May 15–16, 1874.

26. "A Tribute to Tom Paine," *New York Times,* January 30, 1875, 1.

27. Anderson, 153; "A Letter from Mrs. Ernestine L. Rose," *Boston Investigator,* February 10, 1875, 8.

28. "The Investigator Society," *Boston Investigator,* December 6, 1876, 6. I changed Susan B. Anthony's remarks to the first-person form, as she would have spoken them.

29. "A Letter from Mrs. Ernestine L. Rose," *Boston Investigator,* February 8, 1871, 2; "A Letter from England," *Boston Investigator,* February 9, 1876, 1.

30. "A Letter from Mrs. E. L. Rose," *Boston Investigator,* December 23, 1874, 2.

31. Stanton, Anthony, and Gage, eds., *History of Woman Suffrage,* vol. 1: 98–99, Gutenberg E-book.

32. Ernestine L. Rose, "Letter to the Editor," *Boston Investigator,* April 30, 1856, cited in Doress-Worters, 208.

33. Ernestine L. Rose is quoted by Henrietta Muller, *Women's Penny Paper,* February 2, 1889, 1, in Anderson, 167.

34. *Report of a General Conference of Liberal Thinkers, for the Discussion of Matters Pertaining to the Religious Needs of our Time,* June 13–14, 1878, South Place Chapel, London, https://www.google.com/books, 26–27, 31, 41–63.

35. *Liberal Thinkers,* 27.

36. Mary Elizabeth Burtis, *Moncure Conway, 1832–1907* (New Brunswick: Rutgers University Press, 1952), 171.

37. Walter Arnstein, *The Bradlaugh Case: Atheism, Sex and Politics among the Late Victorians* (Columbia: Missouri University Press, 1983), 20, 38, 117–118.

38. *Liberal Thinkers,* 27.

39. "Blasphemy Laws Still Exist in the United States," *Centre for Inquiry Canada,* August 4, 2015, https://www.centreforinquiry.ca.

40. *Liberal Thinkers,* 62–63.

41. "*Unitarian Herald,*" in *Boston Investigator,* July 31, 1878, 3, cited in Anderson, 158.

42. Sidney Warren, *American Freethought, 1860–1914* (New York, Gordian Press, 1966), 228–229, cited in Doress-Worters, 38; Susan Jacoby, *Freethinkers: A History of American Secularism* (New York: Metropolitan Books, 2004), 125–129.

43. Ernestine L. Rose, Speech, "*Congrès International des Sociétés des Amis de la Paix,*" 26 septembre–1 octobre., 1878 (Paris: Imprimerie Nationale, 1880), https://www.cnum.cnam.fr/CG/fpage.cgi. My translation from the French.

44. Carol Faulkner, "How Did an International Agenda Shape the American Women's Rights Movement, 1840–1869?" September 2012, Schlesinger Library, Radcliffe Institute, Harvard University, ProQuest Ebrary.

45. Katherine M. Marino, "The International History of the U.S. Suffrage Movement," https://www.nps.gov/articles/the-internationalist-history-of -the-us-suffrage-movement.htm.

46. Charles Bradlaugh is quoted in J. P. Mendum, "Obituary for William E. Rose," *Boston Investigator*, February 22, 1882, in Doress-Worters, 355.

47. Mendum, "Obituary," 355–356.

Epilogue

"I Have Lived"

Ernestine Rose would live for another ten years after the death of her husband—years marked by failing health and increasing isolation. Quiet and unassuming, William Rose had been her rock who had dedicated his life to her and to their causes. He had sustained her during times when her words had fallen on deaf ears or had been met with scorn or hostility. A successful businessman, he had been happy to provide her with "the means of making her extensive tours, so that through his sense of justice she was enabled to preach the Gospel of Woman's Rights, Anti-Slavery, and Free Religion without money and without price."[1] Rose described her late husband to a visitor this way: "Our lives were as one. He rejoiced in my work, and gladly furnished the means for my journeys and lectures."[2]

Just as Ernestine Rose was a trailblazing activist and orator, William Rose was also a trailblazer—as an abolitionist, freethinker and husband, who by dedicating himself to supporting his wife's work, enabled her to bring about significant reforms. Freethinkers honored William Rose by hanging his portrait in the Paine Memorial Building, alongside those of Ernestine Rose, Robert Owen and Thomas Paine.

Rose's friends rallied to her support and did their best to alleviate some of her grief and loneliness. Susan B. Anthony and Elizabeth Cady Stanton visited her in December 1882. Stanton's description of their visit in *History of Woman Suffrage* is quite different from what she wrote in her diary. She wrote in the first work: "We found our noble coadjutor, though in delicate health, pleasantly situated in the heart of London, as deeply interested as ever in the struggles of the hour."[3] In her diary, Stanton was more candid about her concerns for Rose. While she had presented a largely upbeat description of her in a book intended for wide distribution, she noted in her private journal:

I called on Ernestine Rose and found her very feeble. I sat with her for an hour talking over the past. She was as bright, witty and sarcastic as ever. It is sad to be as alone in the world as she is with not one soul with a drop of her blood in their veins living, not one life-long friend at hand on whom she can call. I urged her to return to America. She said she would like to do so, but feared she had not the strength enough for the voyage.[4]

After Susan B. Anthony had visited her in March 1883, she wrote in her diary: "Rose threw her arms around my neck and said, 'O that my heart would break now and you might close my eyes, dear Susan!'" Anthony, like Stanton, was struck by Rose's extreme isolation and loneliness following her husband's death. After another visit with Rose in October of that year, Anthony observed that Rose was perhaps not as alone as she had earlier imagined: "Last evening at Mrs. Rose's, I met the daughter of Charles Bradlaugh [editor of the *National Reformer*], a talented young woman, whom the college refused to admit to botany lectures because of her father's atheism." This was Alice Bradlaugh. Her sister, Hypatia Bradlaugh, later wrote that Ernestine Rose was "very fond of my sister [Alice], who visited her frequently." Both became close friends with Rose.[5]

Rose had a circle of close friends on both sides of the Atlantic. She continued to send letters during the 1880's to Horace Seaver and Josiah P. Mendum, editors of the *Boston Investigator*. The *Investigator* published almost all of them, including this note from Rose in December 1883: "I am oftentimes so ill that it is quite impossible for me to write, and even now I can hardly hold the pen . . . In my very lonely condition, the dear old *Investigator*, which I value very highly, helps to keep me alive, if I may call my present inaction life, which I don't, for action only is life."[6]

Rose continued to closely follow events in America and to write to the *Investigator.* She sent a letter to Mendum in June 1886, in anticipation of Independence Day:

> I am deeply interested in all the affairs of America. May the Great Republic, 'now known and honored throughout the earth,' as Daniel Webster said of its beautiful Starry Flag, always and forever be the home and asylum of Liberty, mental and political, and may kings and tyrants soon learn from its grand example that the only true or legitimate power to rule is in the People and not in any pretended 'right Divine.' But I really didn't intend . . . to give you a Fourth of July oration, yet as that great day is drawing nigh, my thought is of the famous land beyond the sea where 'the eagle screams' for equal rights for men and women.[7]

Though she became more physically frail, her mind remained sharp and she kept up her correspondence with friends. Rose wrote to Reverend Edward

F. Strickland, a progressive American clergyman who had requested her autograph and photo. In her response, she enclosed her photograph and a copy of a lecture she had given on women's rights, adding, "In a few days, I will return to London where I now live because I am too ill to return to dear America." Charles Bradlaugh wrote in the *National Reformer* the following year: "[Rose] is now, in her 77th year, as outspoken and faithful to her recognition of truth as she was half a century ago."[8]

Her last decade was marked by the death of many of her closest friends—Mathilde Anneke (1884), Alice Bradlaugh (1888), Horace Seaver (1889), Josiah Mendum (1891), and Charles Bradlaugh (1891). After one of her friends, Joseph Mazzini Wheeler, author of a book on freethinkers, had visited her in Brighton in October 1889, he wrote of her:

> Now in her 79th year, she suffers much, and is only able to go out and enjoy the sea-air by means of a bath-chair. But she still retains her keen interest in all Liberal movements, and her fine face is lighted up when she speaks of America, of which she is proud to own herself a citizen, and recalls the memories of the days when her voice was a trumpet-call to the soldiers of freedom . . . Seated at the window . . . she was ready to give (coppers) to any musician or needy person who may pass . . . She is ever mindful of others, and her chief pleasure is in ministering to their wants.[9]

Rose always had an outward focus in life as she dedicated herself to her many interconnected causes—human rights, racial equality, women's rights, freethought and religious freedom—and she preferred to not focus on her personal life. At a Thomas Paine Celebration in 1856, she had expressed her philosophy of life this way:

> I have often been told, 'Your principles are very well to live by, but will they prepare you how to die?' . . . All we need is the right principles to live by, and the rest will take care of itself . . . This senseless talk of teaching man how to die while he is left utterly ignorant [of] how to live—to make the world wiser, better, and happier for his living in it—is as ridiculous as it is pernicious, for it diverts man's attention from life and its duties, and prevents him from acquiring a knowledge of his being, the laws that govern him, and the relation he sustains to his fellow man.[10]

She was not concerned about dying but her greatest fear was that a religious zealot might try to convert her to Christianity against her wishes. Rose had always remained true to her convictions, to her "heresies," as she liked to call them, even as they caused her to be maligned. Her friend Hypatia Bradlaugh Bonner wrote about Rose's concerns: "Mrs. Rose had greatly dreaded that during her last illness she would be invaded by religious persons who might make her unsay the convictions of her whole life when her brain was weakened by illness and she did not know what she was doing." To prevent this, Rose arranged for Hypatia Bonner to be with her when she fell seriously ill.[11] In her will, she requested that her executors "not permit [her] body to be taken into any Chapel or Church but carry out [her] funeral in like manner . . . as that of [her] late husband."

Rose left her gold watch to Ernest Mendum, her namesake (son of Josiah Mendum). She left instructions for her estate to be divided among her three half-nieces, the granddaughters of her father and his second wife: Jeannette Pulvermacher (née Morgenstern), Ernestine Radziejewski (née Morgenstern) and Bertha Sigismund (née Morgenstern). The fact that Rose chose to leave her estate to her nieces, and gave their addresses in her will, revealed that she had some contact with her Polish family.[12]

Ernestine Rose remained faithful to her beliefs to the end. When she went out for fresh air in Brighton on August 1, 1892, Rose suffered a stroke. She died three days later on August 4. According to her attendants who were by her side—Dr. Washington Epps and Miss Byrne—she died peacefully, "untroubled by any thoughts of religion."[13]

Following Rose's wishes, George Jacob Holyoake, successor to Robert Owen as leader of the Owenite socialist movement in England, gave the eulogy for Ernestine Rose at a graveside service in Highgate Cemetery. Many of Rose's friends as well as her great-niece, Anna Pulvermacher Allinson, attended the service.

Holyoake spoke of the deep relationship of William and Ernestine Rose: " . . . [William's] regard for his wife exceeded anything of the kind I have ever known, and her affection for him was such that though she had numerous personal friends in every great city of America, she would never leave England, where her husband lay buried. Her desire was to be in the same grave, and today, in this spot, her desire is fulfilled." Holyoake's words provide a clear explanation for Rose's decision to remain in England. She had earlier written that her financial concerns and her ill health had made it difficult for her to move to America.

In praising Rose's many contributions, Holyoake first mentioned her work as an abolitionist: "She even went into the slave states pleading for Negro freedom. She was threatened with tar and feathers. She answered that 'for the sake of humanity she would risk the tar.'" Holyoake noted her other important achievements. He spoke of her work as an Owenite: " . . . She became the most influential advocate of [Owen's] views in that country [America]"; and of her work as a women's rights and freethought advocate:

She had the fire of Judith in her, and her passion was to see women possess civil and social equality, and to inspire women and men with self-helping sense, not taking religion, politics, or social ideas secondhand from their 'pastors and masters' but choosing principles of belief, government, and conduct for themselves . . . Mrs. Rose took truth for authority, not authority for truth.[14]

While historians have emphasized Rose's accomplishments as an advocate of women's rights, Holyoake rightly focused on her equally important contributions to racial equality and to what Rose called "mental freedom"—her belief that each person needs to find truth for himself and to reject all forms of authoritarianism. Freedom of expression, she stressed, was essential to democracy. Rose spoke out against blasphemy laws, which criminalized atheism, and against the Comstock Law, which made it illegal to disseminate information about birth control.

Holyoake said that Rose "had the fire of Judith in her," comparing her to a Jewish biblical heroine who saved her people by murdering the general Holofernes. Holyoake's ironic choice of words to describe Rose, given that they were both freethinkers, emphasized her Jewish identity. Rose had a complicated relationship with Judaism: she disavowed all religious faith, yet retained Judaism's most important ethical precepts. Rabbi Sally Priesand, the first female ordained rabbi in America, remarked: "Social justice is one of the foundations of our tradition, and anyone raised with Jewish values knows the importance of *tikkun olam.*"[15]

Whenever Rose encountered anti-Semitism she forcefully denounced it, while defending Judaism and Jewish people, as in her letters to Horace Seaver. She was a champion of Jewish rights—as she was of all human rights—vehemently condemning the Mortara Affair in Italy. Rose, along with Rabbi David Einhorn and Michael Heilprin, was one of the earliest Jewish abolitionists and social justice activists in America. She can be considered a forerunner of twentieth-century female activists in the civil rights and women's movements. As a freethinker, Rose saw the dangers of religious fundamentalism and of other forms of authoritarianism. She stressed the importance of secularism in civic life, a principle that America's Founding Fathers had advocated.

Many contemporary women's rights activists paid tribute to Ernestine Rose. Susan B. Anthony kept a portrait of Rose on the wall of her study. She wrote of her: "Bravest and fearless of all women—Mrs. Rose," and "after Frances Wright, the earliest advocate of woman's enfranchisement in America."[16] Elizabeth Cady Stanton said movingly of Rose: "For half a century, as a public speaker, her eloquent voice was heard on both continents, she having taken an active part in all the great progressive movements of our day . . . How much of the freedom we now enjoy may be due to this noble Polish woman cannot be estimated, for moral influences are too subtle for measurement . . . "[17] Rose undoubtedly influenced Stanton to write *The*

Woman's Bible (1895), which contended that religion had deterred the social advance of women.[18]

Lillie Devereux Blake, a women's rights advocate of the next generation, said of Rose: "I never heard her speak but once, and she was then an old lady in frail health, but she thrilled the audience by the electric force of her words, and her dark eyes flashed as her voice rose in the fiery earnestness of her eloquence."[19] Blake's tribute, like that of many others, emphasized the extraordinary power of Rose's spoken words, even in her old age.

The *Boston Investigator* wrote a long, glowing tribute to Rose that concluded with these words: "[Rose] set a heroic example to her sex, and labored for the human race with noble purpose and unselfish aim . . . Such a life as she lived is to be imitated by those who would add to the glory of humanity."[20]

Given Ernestine Rose's many achievements and her fame in America during much of her lifetime, how surprising it is then, that for more than half a century after her death she was forgotten. A veil of silence fell over her memory in America and Europe. Journalist Henry Lewis wrote in the *Forward* in 1927 that he couldn't understand "the oblivion which has engulfed the memory of this remarkable woman . . . I doubt whether one American Jew in ten thousand has ever heard of her."[21] The *Boston Investigator*'s 1871 prediction had come true: "Mrs. Rose, though one of the oldest, ablest and most deserving advocates of the Rights of Women, is not a Christian, and for this reason is not appreciated by her sex as her merits deserve. She will be, however, in about a hundred years!"[22]

As a Jew, a freethinker and a foreigner in a largely conservative Christian, nativist country, Rose was too outspoken and progressive for her era. Beginning in the mid-twentieth century, however, with the women's rights and civil rights movements and with growing concerns about religious fundamentalism, many have begun to recognize Ernestine Rose's importance.[23]

In his eulogy, Holyoake mentioned some words that Rose had said near the end of her life: "It is no longer necessary for me to live. I can do nothing now. But I have lived."[24] Rose, a "volunteer soldier in the cause of Truth," had given meaning to her life by contributing to many progressive reform movements. She found a life of inaction understandably difficult to tolerate during her last years. Her words, "I have lived," showed her pride and satisfaction regarding all that she had accomplished during her long career.

One of her greatest accomplishments was her work with other abolitionists to help end slavery in America and to demand passage of the Thirteenth Amendment. Unfortunately, racism continues today to plague the nation.

When Rose had begun advocating in 1836 for passage of the Married Women's Property Act, married women were, "in the eyes of the law, classified with minors and idiots."[25] When she married, a woman lost all rights to property she had inherited, to wages she earned, and to guardianship of her children. In 1860, Rose commented on the remarkable changes she had observed in women's lives since those early years of activism: "—the change in public opinion, the constantly widening and increasing avenues of industry for woman, in the mercantile, mechanical, and professional avocations . . . Perhaps nowhere is the change more perceptible than in the press."[26] Higher educational opportunities for women greatly expanded. While women had previously been limited to the domestic sphere, they made major strides in the labor market by the end of the 19th century, although they received a lower salary than men.[27] American women would not win the right to vote, however, until 1920.

Ernestine Rose was too bold, too forward-thinking to be appreciated during her lifetime. In the twenty-first century, we are coming to appreciate her wit, her powerful words and her devotion to the cause of freedom and democracy. Rose expressed it this way:

> In every reform ever introduced . . . a few disinterested, devoted champions . . . sowed the seed and carefully tended the growth of the young plant until it was strong enough to brave the storm and bear fruit . . . until a strong public opinion had been created in its favor: the harvest was ripe.[28]

Our generation of men and women, and the generations that follow, are the beneficiaries of Rose's hard work and dedication. The harvest is ripe.

NOTES

1. "Ernestine L. Rose," in Elizabeth Cady Stanton, Susan B. Anthony, Matilda Joslyn Gage, eds., *History of Woman Suffrage,* vol. 1: 98, Gutenberg E-book.

2. Henrietta Muller, *Women's Penny Paper*, February 2, 1889, 1, cited in Bonnie S. Anderson, *The Rabbi's Atheist Daughter: Ernestine Rose, International Feminist Pioneer* (Oxford University Press, 2017), 167.

3. Elizabeth Cady Stanton, "Reminiscences," *History of Woman Suffrage,* vol. 3: 940, Gutenberg E-book.

4. Elizabeth Cady Stanton, *Elizabeth Cady Stanton as Revealed in her Letters, Diary and Reminiscences*, vol. 2: 201 (New York: Harper and Brothers, 1922).

5. Ida Husted Harper, *Life and Work of Susan B. Anthony*, vol. 2: 554 (Indianapolis: Bowen-Merrill, 1898–1908); Hypatia Bradlaugh, "Mrs. Ernestine L. Rose," *National Reformer*, August 14, 1892.

6. "Ernestine L. Rose," *Boston Investigator,* December 19, 1883, 5.

7. "Ernestine L. Rose," *Boston Investigator,* June 3, 1886.

8. Ernestine L. Rose, Letter to Rev. Edward F. Strickland, August 30, 1887, American Jewish Archives, Klau Library, Cincinnati, Ohio; "Mrs. Ernestine L. Rose," *Boston Investigator,* March 16, 1887, 4 [a reprint from the *National Reformer*].

9. Joseph Mazzini Wheeler, "A Visit to Two Veteran Freethinkers in England," *Boston Investigator*, October 9, 1889, 2.

10. Ernestine L. Rose, "Speech at the Thomas Paine Celebration, January 28, 1856," in Paula Doress-Worters, ed., *Mistress of Herself: Speeches and Letters of Ernestine L. Rose, Early Women's Rights Leader* (New York: The Feminist Press, 2008), 206.

11. Bradlaugh, "Mrs. Ernestine L. Rose."

12. "Last Will and Testament of Ernestine Louise Rose," cited in Yuri Suhl, *Ernestine Rose and the Battle for Human Rights* (New York: Reynal, 1959), 279.

13. "Last Will," 279.

14. George Jacob Holyoake, "Eulogy for Ernestine L. Rose," August 8, 1892, in Doress-Worters, 357–358.

15. Adrienne Wigdortz Anderson, "100 Years On: The Jewish Suffragists who Helped Women Win the Right to Vote," *Jewish Journal*, August 14, 2020, https://jewishjournal.com/news/united-states/320383/100-years-on-the-jewish-suffragists-who-helped-women-win-the-right-to-vote/.

16. Susan B. Anthony wrote this message on a copy of Rose's Speech at the 1853 Hartford Bible Convention, quoted in Anderson, 89; "Ernestine L. Rose," in Stanton, Anthony, and Gage, eds., *History of Woman Suffrage,* vol. 3:120, Gutenberg E-book.

17. Elizabeth Cady Stanton, "Tribute to Ernestine L. Rose," *Twenty-fifth Annual Convention of the National American Woman Suffrage Association,* January 16–19, 1893, in Doress-Worters, 360.

18. Earl Conrad, "Ernestine Rose: Queen of the Platform," *The Jewish Fraternalist*, April 1947, 5.

19. Lillie Devereux Blake, "Ernestine L. Rose," *Atchison Globe*, October 15, 1890.

20. "Ernestine L. Rose," *Boston Investigator,* August 17, 1892, 6.

21. Henry Lewis, "Ernestine Rose—First Jewish Advocate of Women's Rights," *Forward*, June 19, 1927.

22. "Ernestine L. Rose," *Boston Investigator,* March 22, 1871, 6.

23. There is, for example, an Ernestine L. Rose Society at Brandeis University.

24. "Eulogy," in Doress-Worters, 358.

25. Stanley R. Brav, "The Jewish Woman, 1861–1865," *American Jewish Archives Journal* 17, no. 1 (1965): 74.

26. Ernestine L. Rose, "Woman's Rights," *Boston Investigator,* April 11, 1860, in Doress-Worters, 259.

27. Jone Johnson Lewis, "A Brief History of Women in Higher Education," March 25, 2019, https://www.thoughtco.com /history-women-higher-ed; Melvin Kranzberg and Michael T. Hannan, "Women in the Workforce," https://www.britannica.com.

28. Ernestine L. Rose, "Authoresses to the Rescue," *The Revolution*, December 28, 1868, 43.

Bibliography

Anderson, Adrienne Wigdortz. "100 Years On: The Jewish Suffragists Who Helped Women Win the Right to Vote." *Jewish Journal*, August 14, 2020. https://jewishjournal.com/culture/320383.

Anderson, Bonnie S. *The Rabbi's Atheist Daughter: Ernestine Rose, International Feminist Pioneer.* New York: Oxford University Press, 2017.

Arnstein, Walter. *The Bradlaugh Case: Atheism, Sex and Politics among the Late Victorians.* Columbia: Missouri University Press, 1983.

Barnard, L[emuel] E. "Ernestine L. Rose." *The Liberator*, May 16, 1856.

Berenson, Barbara F. *Massachusetts in the Woman Suffrage Movement.* Charleston: The History Press, 2018.

Berkowitz, Sandra J. and Amy C. Lewis. "Debating Anti-Semitism: Ernestine Rose vs. Horace Seaver in the *Boston Investigator, 1863–1864.*" *Communication Quarterly* 46, no. 4 (Fall 1998): 457–471.

Blight, David W. *Race and Reunion: The Civil War in American Memory.* Cambridge: The Belknap Press of Harvard University, 2001.

Brav, Stanley R. "The Jewish Woman, 1861–1865." *American Jewish Archives*, 17, no. 1 (1965): 34–75.

Burrows, Edwin G., and Mike Wallace. *Gotham: A History of New York City to 1898.* New York: Oxford University Press, 1999.

Burtis, Mary Elizabeth. *Moncure Conway, 1832–1907.* New Brunswick: Rutgers University Press, 1952.

Cahen, Isidore. "Un Champion israélite de l'Émancipation féminine." *Archives israélites* 53 (1892): 317–318.

Case, Holly. *The Age of Questions.* Princeton, NJ: Princeton University Press, 2018.

Ceniza, Sherry. *Walt Whitman and 19ᵗʰ Century Women Reformers.* Tuscaloosa: University of Alabama Press, 1998: 140–180.

Center for the History of Medicine, Countway Library of Medicine. "Sir Francis Galton." https://chm@hms.harvard.edu.

Centre for Inquiry Canada. "Blasphemy Laws Still Exist in the United States," August 4, 2015. https://www.centreforinquiry.ca.

Conrad, Earl. "Ernestine Rose: Queen of the Platform." *The Jewish Fraternalist* (April 1947): 5.

Cook, Lisa Connelly. "The Radical Egalitarian Agenda of the First National Woman's Rights Convention of 1850." MA thesis, Clark University, 1998. Worcester Women's History Project. https://www.wwhp.org.

Corbin, Caroline F. "Woman's Rights in America, 1848–1908." New York: New York State Association Opposed to Woman Suffrage, 1913.

D'Costa, Krystal. "A Right to Be Clean: Sanitation and the Rise of New York City's Water Towers." February 18, 2013. https://www.blogs.scientificamerican.com/anthropology-in-practice/a-right-to-be-clean-sanitation-and-the-rise-of-new-york-citys-water-towers/.

D'Héricourt, Jenny P. "Madame Rose." *La Revue Philosophique et Religieuse* 5: 129–139. Paris: Bureaux de la Revue, 1856. For an English translation, "Madame Rose: A Life of Ernestine L. Rose as told to Jenny P. d'Héricourt," *Journal of Women's History* 15, no. 1 (Spring 2003): 183–201. Ed., Paula Doress-Worters; trans., Jane Pincus, Mei Mei Ellerman, Ingrid Kislink, Erica Hurth, and Allen J. Worters, with Karen Offen.

Davis, Paulina W. *A History of the National Woman's Rights Movement.* New York: Source Books, 1970 [1871].

Dawidowicz, Lucy S. *The Golden Tradition: Jewish Life and Thought in Eastern Europe.* Boston: Beacon Press, 1967.

De Tocqueville, Alexis. *Democracy in America.* Translated by Arthur Goldhammer. New York: Library of America, 2004 [1835–1840].

Deutscher, Isaac. "The Non-Jewish Jew." *The Non-Jewish Jew and other Essays.* London: Verso, 2017.

Diedrich, Maria. *Love Across Color Lines: Ottilie Assing and Frederick Douglass.* New York: Hill and Wang, 1999.

Diner, Hasia R. *The Jews of the United States, 1654–2000.* Berkeley: University of California Press, 2004.

Dixon-Fyle, Joyce. *Female Writers' Struggle for Rights and Education for Women in France (1848–1871).* New York: Lang, 2006.

Doress-Worters, Paula, ed. *Mistress of Herself: Speeches and Letters of Ernestine L. Rose, Early Women's Rights Leader.* New York: The Feminist Press, 2008.

Douglass, Frederick. "What to the Slave is the Fourth of July?" July 5, 1852, https://www.democracynow.org/2021/7/5/james_earl_jones_frederick_douglass_july4.

———. *Life and Times of Frederick Douglass.* New York: Library of America, 1994 [(London: Christian Age Office, 1882].

DuBois, Ellen Carol. "Ernestine Rose's Jewish Origins and the Varieties of Euro-American Emancipation in 1848." In Sklar, Kathryn Kish and James Brewer Stewart, eds. *Women's Rights and Transatlantic Antislavery in the Era of Emancipation.* New Haven, CT: Yale University Press, 2007: 279–298.

Edison, Thomas A. "The Philosophy of Thomas Paine." Thomas Paine Friends, Inc. https://www.thomas-paine-friends.org/edison-thomas_essay-on-paine.htm, 1–4.

Emerson, Ralph Waldo. *Selected Writings.* Edited by William H. Gilman. New York: Signet Classics, 2003.

Engseth, Ellen. "Mathilde Franziska Anneke." *Encyclopedia of Milwaukee.* https://www.emke.uwm.edu/entry/mathilde-franziska-anneke.

Faulkner, Carol. "How Did an International Agenda Shape the American Women's Rights Movement, 1840–1869?" September 2012. Schlesinger Library, Radcliffe Institute, Harvard University, ProQuest Ebrary.

Foner, Philip S., ed. *Frederick Douglass on Women's Rights*. Westport: Greenwood Press, 1976.

Fraser, Arvonne S. "Becoming Human: The Origins and Development of Women's Human Rights." *Human Rights Quarterly* 21, no. 4 (November 1999): 872.

Fuller, Margaret. *Woman in the Nineteenth Century*. New York: Greeley & McElrath, 1845.

Garrison, Wendell Phillips, and Francis Jackson Garrison. *William Lloyd Garrison, the Story of His Life, Told by his Children. New York: The Century Company, 1885–1889.*

Giladi, Ben. *A Tale of One City: Piotrykow-Trybunalski*. New York: Shengold, 1991. https://archive.org/details/nybc314221.

Ginzberg, Lori D. "Re-viewing the First Wave." *Feminist Studies* 28, no. 2 (Summer 2002). Gale General OneFile.

———. "The Heathen Wing: Reflections on Secular Jewish Traditions." *Bridges* (Summer 1998): 7–14.

Gjelten, Tom. "Can America's 'Civil Religion' Still Unite the Country?" *All Things Considered*, NPR, April 12, 2021. http://www.npr.org/2021/04/12.

Gray, Carole. "Nineteenth-Century Women of Freethought." *Free Inquiry* 15, no. 2 (Spring 1995). Gale Document: GALEA16871567.

Guelzo, Allen C. "Emancipation and the Quest for Freedom," *The Civil War Remembered*. https://www.nps.gov/articles/emancipation-and-the-quest-for-freedom.htm.

Harper, Frances Ellen Watkins. "We Are All Bound up Together." Address given at the Eleventh National Women's Rights Convention in New York City, 1866. https://www.blackpast.org/african-american-history/speeches-african-american-history/1866-frances-ellen-watkins-harper-we-are-all-bound-together/.

Harper, Ida Husted. *The Life and Work of Susan B. Anthony*. 3 vols. Indianapolis: Bowen-Merrill, 1898–1908.

Holmes, David L. "The Founding Fathers, Deism and Christianity." Encyclopedia Britannica, December 21, 2006. https://www.britannica.com/topic/The-Founding-Fathers-Deism-and-Christianity-1272214.

Hone, Philip. *Diary* (1828–1851). Edited by Bayard Tuckerman. 2 vols. New York: Dodd, Mead and Company, 1889. https://archive.org.

Jacoby, Susan. *Freethinkers: A History of American Secularism.* New York: Metropolitan Books, 2004.

Johnson, Linck C. "Reforming the Reformers: Emerson, Thoreau, and the Sunday Lectures at Amory Hall, Boston." *ESQ* 37 (1991): 235–289.

Kaplan, Mordecai M. *Judaism as a Civilization: Toward a Reconstruction of American Jewish Life.* Philadelphia: Jewish Publication Society, 1981.

Kertzer, David I. *The Kidnapping of Edgardo Mortara*. New York: Vintage Books, 1998.

Kolmerten, Carol A. *The American Life of Ernestine L. Rose.* Syracuse, NY: Syracuse University Press, 1999.

Korn, Bertram W. "The Rabbis and the Slavery Question." *American Jewry and the Civil War*, 15–31. New York: Atheneum, 1970.

Kraditor, Aileen S. *Up From the Pedestal: Selected Writings in the History of American Feminism.* Chicago: Quadrangle, 1968.

Kranzberg, Melvin, and Michael T. Hannan. "Women in the Workforce." https://www.britannica.com.

Lepore, Jill. *These Truths: A History of the United States.* New York: W.W. Norton, 2018.

Lewis, Henry. "Ernestine Rose—First Jewish Advocate of Women's Rights." *Forward*, June 19, 1927.

Lewis, Jone Johnson. "A Brief History of Women in Higher Education," March 25, 2019. https://www.thoughtco.com /history-women-higher-ed; Melvin.

Lincoln, Abraham. *The Collected Works of Abraham Lincoln.* Edited by Roy Basler. 9 vols. New Brunswick: Rutgers University Press, 1953.

Lindemann, A.S. *Esau's Tears: Modern Anti-Semitism and the Rise of the Jews.* New York: Cambridge University Press, 1997.

Marino, Katherine M. "The International History of the U.S. Suffrage Movement." https://www.nps.gov/articles/the-internationalist-history-of-the-us-suffrage-movement.htm.

McPherson, James M. *Battle Cry of Freedom: The Civil War Era.* New York: Oxford University Press, 1988.

National Archives. "The Freedmen's Bureau." https://www.archives.gov/research/african-americans/freedmens-bureau.

Oakes, James. *The Radical and the Republican: Frederick Douglass, Abraham Lincoln and the Triumph of Antislavery Politics.* New York: Norton, 2007.

Offen, Karen. "A Nineteenth-Century French Feminist Rediscovered: Jenny d'Héricourt, 1809–1875." *Signs* 13, no.1 (Fall 1987):144–158.

Owen, Robert. *The Catechism of the New Moral World.* London: H. Hetherington, 1830.

———. *The Social Bible: an Outline of the Rational System of Society.* London: H. Hetherington, 1840.

Parker, Theodore. *A Sermon of Mexican War, Preached at the Melodeon*, June 7, 1846. Boston: I.R. Butts, 1846.

Parush, Iris, and Ann Brener. "Readers in Cameo: Women Readers in Jewish Society of Nineteenth-Century Eastern Europe." *Prooftexts* 14, no. 1 (January 1994): 1–23.

Phillips, Wendell. "Shall women have the right to vote?" Address given in Worcester, MA, 1851. Worcester Women's History Project. https://www.wwhp.org.

Pula, James S. "'The Noblest Deed in a Hundred Years': Polish Participation in the Antislavery Crusade." *Polish American Studies* 75, no. 1 (Spring 2018): 1–8.

Reps, John W. *Washington on View: The Nation's Capital since 1790.* Chapel Hill: University of North Carolina Press, 1991.

Richardson, Marilyn, ed. *Maria W. Stewart, America's First Black Woman Political Writer: Essays and Speeches.* Bloomington: Indiana University Press, 1987.

Rose, Ernestine L. *A Defence of Atheism: a Lecture Delivered in Mercantile Hall, Boston, April 10, 1861.* Boston: J. P. Mendum, 1881.

———. *An Address on Woman's Rights Delivered in Cochituate Hall, Boston, October 19, 1851.* Boston: J. P. Mendum, 1851.

Sarna, Jonathan D. *American Judaism: A History.* New Haven: Yale University Press, 2005.

Schappes, Morris U. "Ernestine L. Rose: Her Address on the Anniversary of West Indian Emancipation." *Journal of Negro History* 34, no. 3 (July 1949): 344–355.

———. "To Be Included." *Morning Freiheit*, March 13, 1948.

———. *A Documentary History of the Jews in the United States, 1654–1875.* New York: Schocken, 1971.

———. *The Jews in the United States: a Pictorial History, 1654 to the Present.* New York: Citadel Press, 1958.

Stanton, Elizabeth Cady, and Susan B. Anthony. *Selected Papers of Elizabeth Cady Stanton and Susan B. Anthony.* Edited by Ann D. Gordon. New Brunswick: Rutgers University Press, 1997.

Stanton, Elizabeth Cady, Susan B. Anthony, and Matilda Joslyn Gage, eds. *History of Woman Suffrage,* 4 vols. 1881,1886, 1902. Gutenberg E-book.

Stanton, Elizabeth Cady. *Elizabeth Cady Stanton as Revealed in her Letters, Diary and Reminiscences.* New York: Harper and Brothers, 1922.

Suhl, Yuri. *Ernestine Rose and the Battle for Human Rights.* New York: Reynal, 1959.

Thoreau, Henry David. *The Writings of Henry David Thoreau.* Edited by Horace Elisha Scudder et al. Boston: Houghton Mifflin Company, 1893.

Traubel, Horace. *With Walt Whitman in Camden.* Carbondale: Southern Illinois University Press, 1982.

Underwood, Sara A. *Heroines of Free Thought.* New York: C. P. Somerby, 1876: 255–281.

Warren, Sidney. *American Freethought, 1860–1914.* New York, Gordian Press, 1966.

Wilentz, Sean. *Chants Democratic: New York City and the Rise of the American Working Class, 1788–1850.* New York: Oxford University Press, 1984.

Index

abolition,18, 31, 34, 38, 41, 45–48, 56,
  58, 64–66, 78, 83, 89, 94; as Rose's
  cause, xi–xiv, 25–26, 33, 36–37,
  39–40, 43–44, 49, 95
Abzug, Bella, 91
Addams, Jane, 119
Albany Register, 62, 69n9, 71n37
Alliance Israélite Universelle, 84
Allinson, Anna Pulvermacher, 126
Amendments (US Constitution):
  First, 90, 118; Thirteenth, 48, 64;
  Fourteenth, 64; Fifteenth, 48, 65–67,
  69n7, 84; Nineteenth, 68
American Equal Rights Association,
  65–66, 69n7, 71n49, 76, 84
American Revolution, xiii, 22, 74
American Woman Suffrage Association,
  67–68, 130n17
Amory Hall Lectures, 22–25, 29n29
Anneke, Mathilde Franziska, 78–79,
  85, 86nn20–22
Anthony, Susan B., xii, xvi n6, 37–41,
  48, 50n23, 51n28, 51n41, 55,
  64–68, 69n10, 72n61, 108, 113, 119,
  121n28, 129n5; and Rose, xv, 30n42,
  45, 50n20, 68, 105n36, 114, 124–
  125; Rose's letters to, xv, 15n53,
  27, 30n51, 68–69, 108, 115, 120n5;
  travels with Rose, 26, 37–38, 42, 99

anticlericalism, 116
anti-Semitism, xii, 67, 84, 91, 95, 100,
  102, 106n41
Assing, Ottilie, 83, 87n35
*Association Internationale des
  Femmes*, 119
Association of All Classes of All
  Nations, 9
atheism, 14n27, 52n60, 89, 98, 104n11,
  105n34, 116, 118, 121n37

Barnard, Lemuel E., 29n21, 29n27,
  30n41, 42, 51n31, 63, 71n38
Beecher, Henry Ward, 63
Bem, Józef, 74
Besant, Annie, 117
Black Codes, 49, 65
Blake, Lillie Devereux, 128
bloomers, 83, 87n37
Bonaparte, Napoleon, 76
Bonner, Hypatia Bradlaugh. *See*
  Bradlaugh, Hypatia
Booth, John Wilkes, 64
Boston Investigator, 22, 114; editors,
  27, 89, 99–100, 116, 119–120; on
  Rose, 22, 25, 27, 63, 75, 108–109,
  125, 128; Rose's letters to, 8,
  14nn35–38, 14n40, 69n3, 79–83,
  95–96, 99–103, 115–116, 124

About the Author

Joyce B. Lazarus is the author of *Geneviève Straus: a Parisian Life* (Brill, 2017), *Hiding in Plain Sight: Eluding the Nazis in Occupied France* (Chicago Review Press, 2012), *In the Shadow of Vichy: The Finaly Affair* (Lang, 2008), *Strangers and Sojourners: Jewish Identity in Contemporary Francophone Fiction* (Lang, 1999), and *Parole aux jeunes* (Heinle & Heinle, 1992). A graduate of Queens College, CUNY (BA) and Harvard University (MA, PhD), she is Professor Emerita of World Languages at Framingham State University. Her research interests include French history and literature, Jewish studies, women's studies and the struggle for human rights.